From

Master Fard Muhammad

HOW TO
EAT
TO LIVE

Book No. 2

By
ELIJAH MUHAMMAD
Messenger of Allah

Published by

Muhammad's Temple of Islam No. 2

7351 South Stony Island Avenue

Chicago, Illinois 60649

Books by Elijah Muhammad

MESSAGE TO THE BLACKMAN IN AMERICA

HOW TO EAT TO LIVE

CONTENTS

CONTENTS

CONTENTS

INTRODUCTION

"O men, eat the lawful and good things
from what is in the earth, and follow not
the footsteps of the devil. Surely he is
an open enemy to you."

Holy Quran 2:168

The wisdom of Allah, given to us in the book "How to Eat to Live," Volume 1, by the Honorable Elijah Muhammad, exhibits the power of the Black man's God, to take a people in the lowest condition of life and by the regulation of their dietary habits, raise them to a higher spiritual and physical condition. "How to Eat to Live," Volume II, will continue this evolution to higher perfection, if we will but "Hear and Obey."

Hear Him - Heed Him, Honor Him, and Obey Him for He alone was chosen and taught and given the keys to our salvation. This book "How to Eat to Live," Volume II, is one of these keys.

Abass Rassoull
National Secretary

GUIDE TO PROPER EATING

CHAPTER ONE

A RETURN TO LONG LIFE

Eat to live to bring about a return to perfection and long life; like Noah and Methuselah, who lived nearly 1000 years of our calendar year (containing 365¼ days).

LONG LIFE IS NOT enjoyed by eating food which will shorten and destroy life. Under this white race of people, we were not taught how to eat to live. They, the white devils, are not here to teach us, the Lost and Found members of the Aboriginal Nation, to live a long life. They were put here to cut short our lives, and for the last 6000 years they have done so.

Eating as beasts eat (Holy Qur-an) all during the day and night will kill us at an early age—very few of the white race have regularity about their eating habits. Our stomachs are worn out in a few years, due to the continuation of trying to digest the food that we eat—some being of the type of foods which we should not dare put into our stomachs.

Poison drinks along with a mixture of good and poison foods have shortened our lives, on the average of about 63½ years at the present time. This is a long way from the 600-800-900 years of life of our fathers.

WE ARE A LONG WAY off from the life of the people on Mars, Who Allah in the Person of Master Fard Muhammad, to Whom Praise is due forever, taught me, lived an average life of the equivalent of 1200 years of our earth calendar. This in fact has been

7

the Original Nation's calendar year ever since God created the Heavens and the Earth, so teaches the Holy Qur-an.

If you want a beautiful appearance, eat the proper food and eat one meal a day. When you are used to eating one meal a day, then eat one meal every other day. Your children may be able to eat two meals per week. This will put them into centuries as Noah and Methuselah.

CHAPTER TWO

HOW TO KEEP FOOD FROM HURTING US

I thank Allah in the Person of Master Fard Muhammad, to Whom Praises are due forever, for bringing to us life and light so that we may be able to enjoy life, and to enjoy that life longer than we have previously enjoyed it.

Many years could be added to our lives if we only knew how to protect our lives from their enemies. As He (meaning Master Fard Muhammad) said to me, food keeps us here; it is essential that we eat food which gives and maintains life. That same food destroys life. Therefore, to keep this food from destroying our lives, we must protect our lives as well as we possibly can from the destruction of food. If we eat the proper food, and eat at the proper time, the food will keep us living a long, long time.

Eating three and four times a day is to your stomach as dripping water is to a stone or iron. The dripping water will eventually wear the stone and iron away. But, just to look at the water, it does not appear powerful enough in its dripping to wear the stone and iron away. It is the same with food; we continuously put it into our stomachs to be digested and eventually it will destroy the stomach. If we let our stomachs rest a while and gain strength, they will last longer in doing a job of digesting food for us.

EAT ONE MEAL a day and eat the food that will not harm you so quickly. You do not have to go into a long detailed knowledge of what foods you have to eat,

9

because the wrong food has already been pointed out to you—foods such as pig, nuts, white flour, meats (of course, we eat some meats), the wrong kind of peas, the wrong kinds of breads, half-cooked breads, too many starchy foods, and too much sweets.

All of these foods destroy us. Bread should be cooked thoroughly and slowly, and if you have plenty of time, cook the bread two or three times and then eat it. Meat should also be cooked two or three times.

Eating great meals of highly seasoned and sugared pastries is definitely not good for us. They most surely will take years of our lives away. You may eat some sweets, but do not make an entire meal of sweets and eat them everyday. Fruit is good for us; we should eat plenty fruits.

To live a long time, eat once every 24 hours or once every 48 hours, if you are able to do so. But, if you have heavy, manual work to do, do not try to eat once every two or three days. And, if you eat once a day, you should fast every month for two or three days. By doing that, there will be no poison left in the body at the end of a year to make you sick even one hour.

I WOULD LIKE for you, who try to live and eat just as this book teaches you, to please send me a letter telling me of the results that you have gained from eating like this article teaches you. I repeatedly teach that the way Allah, in the Person of Master Fard Muhammad, has Taught us to eat will do away with many doctor bills and do away with much maiming of the limbs caused by certain diseases.

Sugar diabetes can be controlled and cured if you only eat right. Stay off of sugar and starchy foods and leave those old, white potatoes alone. Do not eat spaghetti and macaroni at every meal. If you are overweight, do not eat it at any meal, and if you want to live a long time, do not eat it at any meal. Food such as spaghetti and macaroni is processed, not cooked thoroughly, and is hard to digest.

THERE ARE SOME people who claim that they do not receive beneficial results as they should. This is due to wrong mental food that they are eating, which has an effect on their digestive system. To get good results from eating the proper foods, we must have good thoughts.

CHAPTER THREE

LENGTHEN YOUR LIFE

In order to lengthen our lives, we must begin with what we put in us that retains life. Master Fard Muhammad, to Whom Praises are due forever, comes to prolong the lives of the believers.

THERE IS NOT a shadow of a doubt that He (Allah) has taken the proper steps to give us more life in order to have and enjoy the pleasures of life.

He (Allah) said what we eat keeps us here, and the same will take us away. Suppose we ate one-half pound of food a day. At the end of 365 days, we would have eaten 182 1/2 pounds of food per year.

BUT WE EAT more than this amount. For instance, if we live 50 years, we would eat 50 times this much food, at a half pound of food a day.

If we saw 9,000 pounds of raw food piled up before us to consume, we would think that this would be a lot of food to go through our bodies. And we would think that it probably would wear us out to eat that much food in our life time, although we eat tons of food in our life time.

AND IF THIS food is not the proper food to eat, it will wear away our body and cut short three score and 10 years of our lives.

On the average, our people are living around 62 years. This is a very short life to live on an earth that has been here trillions of years. And yet, the average of us cannot live 100 years under the present system of civilization of wickedness.

Master Fard Muhammad, to Whom Praises are due forever, comes to prolong our lives, not to shorten them, by correcting our eating habits to one meal a day instead of three, and by teaching us to eat the proper foods that will not destroy us or shorten our lives to less than 100 years.

His (Allah's) teaching us to eat better food and to cut our eating from three and four times a day to once a day will certainly prolong our lives and increase our beautiful appearance.

A PERSON WHO eats like an animal—three or four times a day and all between meals—cannot retain a beautiful appearance. Eating three times a day and all between meals removes the body's attractiveness in many ways.

We eat meat, but yet meat is not good for us. It becomes a habitual tool. This type of food poisons the blood and goes into the flesh and cannot help but transform and destroy the surface of the flesh.

TAKE, FOR example, a new born baby. Many times its beauty lasts for just a short while and then passes away with its growth. Even in our late twenties and early thirties--because of the life that we live and the frequent eating of poison food--our beautiful appearance begins to pass from us so rapidly, until by our forties and fifties it is nearly completely gone.

Let us eat one meal a day and try getting the best food that we can to eat — vegetables, fruits, pure fresh milk, and pure whole wheat bread, that has been cooked slowly, twice. Doing this will help us to live longer and retain our beautiful appearance much longer.

DO NOT GET into the habit (or if you are already in the habit, stop it) of eating a lot of greasy foods. Regardless of whether the grease is from animal flesh or not, our bodies, by nature, are not made to digest and control grease or lots of fat.

Thousands of minor ailments disappear from us by eating the proper food and at the proper time—one meal a day. He (Allah) teaches us never to eat unless we are hungry. Eating when we are not hungry causes these minor ailments. We are forcing the body to digest food before it is calling for this food.

TAKE THE hog and the dog—they do not live very long, because they eat daily and nightly.

The present civilization is an enemy to right-eousness. Since they were put over us to rule us, they had to find a different way of ruling us other than the good old way of our fathers, who lived several hundreds of years—some nearly a thousand years.

IF WE MET a man today who said he had been on the planet 500 years, we would think that he was lying, because our short lives of less than 100 years, lead us to believe that it is false to think that people can live several hundred years.

It is all in the food and drink that we put into our bodies that lengthens or shortens our lives. Stay away from poison food and drinks—and eat to live.

CHAPTER FOUR

LIVE LONG

What fool is there who does not want to live? Do not even ask a wise person; consult a fool. Even a fool wants to live as long as he can. Well, eat right—one meal a day—and be careful what you eat. The wicked are practicing their wicked way of poisoning the right-eous in their preparation for food and drink so be care-ful what you eat to live.

The Christian race has shortened the lives of na-tions which follow its way of civilization. The so-called American Negroes—the lost and found members of the nation (the Black nation) the first and the last — have been used for experimental purposes. They have suf-fered every evil thing or idea that entered the heart of the slavemaster and his children. This is going on to-day, as never before in a wise and scientific way.

Before the white man was made, the Black man was known to live approximately a thousand years. He ate the right food and ate it at the right time.

Our stomachs are what we make them. If they call for food every two or three hours, we make a habit of feeding them every two or three hours. If we don't make a habit of feeding our stomachs every two or three hours, they will not call for it. We are the God of our own appetite and what we eat.

Remember the prophecy of Jesus: he came to give us life and more life abundantly. He cannot give us more life if we will not protect our life against its enemies.

DO NOT try to eat so many different things. One or two good things are all right, even just milk and bread—but it has been tampered with. It is hard to get a pure glass of milk. It is hard to get a pure piece of whole wheat bread.

They tamper with everything, without any just cause. So, do the best you can and eat one meal a day. You will live longer.

Eat one meal once every twenty-four (24) hours and eat the right food.

Get away from eating a lot of greasy foods and eat more vegetables and fruits.

Do not eat freshly-baked bread or freshly-baked cakes.

EAT ONE MEAL A DAY.

CHAPTER FIVE

DO NOT EAT FORBIDDEN FOOD

The importance of enjoying good health is obeying the teachings of God (Who Came in the Person of Master Fard Muhammad, to Whom Praises is due forever), and that is eating one meal once every 24 hours (one meal a day).

IT IS NOT SO much eating various kinds of food as it is not eating food of any kind too often. Of course, we know the divinely prohibited flesh of the swine is totally forbidden not only to eat, but we are even forbidden to touch or handle the swine. It is punishable under the law of God to eat the swine.

Many of the readers may think that it is all right with God for them to do as they please about His Laws, but we are punished for willfully disobeying the Laws of God, regardless how little the offense may be or how great it may be.

The Christians have been eating the swine for four thousand years. Now, their punishment is total destruction by fire.

THE WHITE RACE was not made to obey the divine law. They were made to oppose it, therefore following after them and doing what they do is getting you the hell. It is no excuse for you. The average so-called Negro thinks it is all right for him to do evil too. But, we are two different people. The so-called American Negro is a divine member lost from the divine circle, while the slave master, who has been his teacher, is an enemy to God, by nature. This is why the Bible teaches you that hell was created for them the day they were made.

Meat will not prolong our lives—it will cut life short. The white race lives on this type of food, meat—animal flesh. The carnivorous beasts and birds who live off of flesh and eat others, have short lives.

VEGETABLES, MILK AND BUTTER are the right foods to eat, when they are pure. But my Dear Brothers, and Sisters do not think that you are getting pure products now from the dairy. Substitutions are added to butter, and much water is added to the milk.

So, do not practice the evil things that the white race is doing, as you are following them now. If they pull off their clothes, you will pull off yours. Do not think you have an option of doing divine law, while you do not? A doom is set for the whole race of them and you will share their doom with them, if you follow eating and drinking intoxicating drinks just because you see them doing such things and going nude in the public (women with dresses above their knees and men wearing just trunks in public).

YOU ARE FOLLOWING one of the filthiest things that even an animal wouldn't follow, by doing such things. White people do this to tempt you to do the same so that you can share hell fire with them.

Eat one meal a day and eat good food.

CHAPTER SIX

PROPER FOODS, SPIRITUALLY AND PHYSICALLY

Eat to live and not to die. The Bible teaches us that God, in the end of the world when He comes, will prolong the people's lives because they have been eating the proper foods, both spiritually and physically. We have to accept it—that is, if we love life and not death.

LIVING LESS than 100 years is a very short life. People in this world admire one who lives to see 90 years (which is a very short life), because of the way they live, eat and drink the wrong foods and drinks. They are surprised to see a person live over 70 years.

Now they want drugs to give you life. Drugs cannot prolong our lives if we are going to eat and drink the wrong food and drink; and drink polluted water. The very water we drink is polluted from filth. We make the water filthy with our own refuse and then turn around calling ourselves cleaning the water to make it fit to drink.

THIS IS NOT because the government is too poor to try and see that its citizens have pure water to drink. It is not because the government is too poor that we have to eat the poor and poison foods. They deliberately cause this drink and food to be impure. Just read what they say about the impure water that we drink out of Lake Michigan and other rivers.

The government permits the deliberate making of alcoholic drinks which it knows are not good for a person who has no limitation on how much of it he drinks. And it deliberately turns out millions and millions of dollars worth of hogs to put on the market, knowing that the hog is poison and was not made for human consumption. They do that to oppose the right foods—the pure foods—that God has given them in abundance.

ANYTIME WE break the law of nature, we are doing harm to ourselves.

The government condemns smoking, but still permits tobacco to be sold to the public. All of this is due to commercializing on that which produces a short life.

Part of the population of the country is being addicted to drugs for the purpose of experimenting with drugs, instead of lenghtening the life by what we eat and drink.

If we know the best food and the best drink, we should try to get them for ourselves and not charge the government with our own foolish acts, just because the government will not stop the sale of such detrimental food and drink.

THE GOVERNMENT could not sell one drop of whiskey unless we buy it. The foolish buyer is the one to be charged.

We have fire, but if we do not use it rightly, it is because of our own foolishness. If you know better, then do better for self.

EAT GOOD FOOD ONCE A DAY.

CHAPTER SEVEN

ABUNDANCY OF LIFE

There are a lot of readers of this book who have many different thoughts and conceptions of this book.

THE MAIN ROOT of this book is to stop you from eating two or three times a day which will prolong your life.

It takes several hours for the proteins and the vitamins in the meal we eat today to be digested and distributed throughout our bodies.

Allah, through the mouths of the Prophets prophesied that when He Comes, He would give us more life—an abundancy of life.

The Book does not teach you how He will extend our lives; how He will make our lives worth living; and how we will rejoice in our lives.

Now, He (Allah) Has Come and He is teaching me to teach you how to live. How to live is to go after that which is essential for us to put in our body as foods which gives life and maintain life in the body.

He (Master Fard Muhammad, to Whom Praises are Due forever), Has taught me how to teach you the best way to extend our lives and that is through the right kind of foods and drinks.

This does not mean we have to eat every herb of the earth; every cattle of the earth, every bird that flies, every domestic fowl, or every piece of fruit that a fruit tree or vine is bearing (as some people think like that). Just a simple food will keep you and me living a long time, if that simple food is good and we eat it only once a day (once every 24 hours).

SOME WEAK people think that they cannot eat once every 24 hours, but our stomach looks to our brain for guidance and looks to our brain to be the "boss" of what it should take in. The stomach does not think for itself. The brain thinks for the stomach.

Allah has given to us and has taught that way of life that is good for us. We can accept it or we can reject it. There are some people who claim that they like the way but they will go ahead and eat that which is not good for them to eat. Then, they get in trouble and they write me and say that they eat once a day but they are sick; they cannot take it. But, do I not know that they are not eating rightly as I teach them that God taught me and that they are not going through 24 hours, eating only one meal? Do they not know that I know they are not carrying out the instructions as they should.

If you get sick, go and fast for three days. This helps kill the poison in your stomach that came from what you ate.

Once every year, we have accumulated enough poison from eating one meal a day to make us sick one day.

I SAY AGAIN, our stomach is not the boss. The brain is the boss. Eat one meal a day and eat good food and do not eat Divinely prohibited food. This is the Word of Allah and His Teachings to prolong our lives.

CHAPTER EIGHT

EXPERIENCE OF VENTURING FROM RIGHT FOOD

The very words, "how to eat to live," is one of the great values in words for us. In these words, we see and we are learning that what we put in us as food, at what time we eat that food, and what type of food we eat, is the key to our life and death. We can use these words, "how to eat to live," to spell how we destroy ourselves.

We must look at these words and teachings of how to eat to live in a more serious way. This is why we suffer so much sickness and death. It is because we do not take how to eat to live in a more serious way. There is no common sickness that cannot be healed by proper eating of the right foods, I, myself, know; having experience of both the right kind of foods and the wrong kind of foods. Allah (God) has Taught me and I tried everything first, myself. I am a self-experienced man and a example of what Allah (God) Taught me. I went for years without eating but one meal a day, and years with eating one meal every three days. So, I know these teachings of Allah (God) are True. Here of late, I have suffered many pains from venturing away from eating the way Allah (God) Taught me. It caused me discomfort, pains, and minor sickness. I deliberately did this, in some instances, so that I will know what happens when you are not following the Teachings. So, as it is written, in all their afflictions, he was afflicted (meaning the Messenger of God).

Eating the proper food once a day will keep you free of sickness for a long time, probably for years. This, I know by self-experience. By eating two or three meals a day, you are inviting some days of discomfort and illness to yourself, and by eating food that does not belong to the body that it is going into, you are making trouble for the body to digest such foods and drinks. We suffer with many ailments in our bodies due to the fact that we are pouring into it food that should not be put in that body (which is the finest nature-built machinery on Earth), and due to the fact that we are not waiting until the strength or power of the poison in the previous meal becomes weak, so that it will be harmless when the strength of a new meal is added. But, twenty-four (24) to forty-eight (48) hours will destroy the poison from the previous meal and make it harmless.

Eat when you have exhausted the previous meal, Allah (GOD) Taught me; then fill up and go until this is exhausted, and then eat another meal. It is logical. As I keep repeating, we dig our own graves, and I may add here that we bring about our own death with our teeth.

Sugar diabetes can be controlled by eating the proper food in such a way that you will never know that you ever had it and you will never see any signs of it. But, you must not continue to pour in the body, power and strength of sugar from your meals that adds to the sugar spilling over in your body. Naturally, it is going to reach out for something or it is going to flood itself after putting too much sugar and starch in the body. But, some of us are so built upon eating what we want that we just cannot abstain from eating these starches and sweet foods. These things are nothing but friends to the sugar diabetic condition. Stay away from it and you will live longer, for diabetes is an evil enemy. It is an enemy to both the flesh and bones of the body.

If you will stop eating foods such as sugar and starchy foods, I know you will do better. I have been self-experienced in everything, and I have been a victim of everything that you are a victim of, except cancer. I do not think that I have cancer; but as I mentioned in this book before, The Last Messenger is not immuned to the sickness and complaints of the common people. He is also to suffer; but yet, as the Book says, the Pleasure of the Lord is with him and that in His Own Good Time, He Will Heal all of us.

So, this is the way Allah (God) has taught me; to heal our sickness and prolong our lives with one meal a day. And, whenever those of you who work in offices and do light work are able, you can eat one meal every forty-eight (48) hours; which would give you more days to your life. Do not say, "I am already so old that I do not have much longer to live anyway." That is true, but if you want to add a few more days to this already distant age you have, you can add to your life by stopping right now from plunging into the grave, and you could add more days to your life.

TIMES OF EATING
AND FASTING

CHAPTER NINE

THE BENEFITS OF EATING ONCE A DAY

Many of my followers write and tell me of the benefit they are receiving from eating one meal a day or one meal every other day. This will produce good results and lengthen our lives. But children should not be forced to fast or to eat once a day or once every other day.

Children and babies should eat at least twice a day. If you are now eating three meals a day and you would like to eat one meal every other day, you should not—all of a sudden—change from three meals a day, every day, to one meal every other day.

FIRST DROP to two meals a day, then one meal a day, and then one meal every other day. It is better to do it this way so that you will not make yourself sick. And if you eat every other day, do not begin your meal with heavy food.

CHAPTER TEN

TRAIN YOURSELF TO EAT
AS ALLAH HAS ADVISED

To keep healthy and strong, and live a long time, on this old earth, ALLAH said to me, in the Person of Master Fard Muhammad, eat one meal a day. Or, one meal every two days, or three days. Do not get frightened, Brothers and Sisters, with your meal hours being lengthened, that you may die or become too hungry.

YOU WILL live and you will not be hungry, after you have gotten your stomach used to the long intervals between meals. Your stomach will take food only when you give it food. And, it won't ask you for any food until that certain hour to which you have accustomed it to being fed.

I used to think like you, before the coming of our God and Saviour, in the Person of Master Fard Muhammad, to Whom Praise is due forever. I began practicing eating one meal every day—nothing between like food. I got used to that within a couple of weeks. And, after a certain length of time, I tried eating once every two days, with nothing between but coffee.

I did not try to pour all of the cream and sugar out of the cream and sugar bowls into the coffee. I sweetened and creamed it the same as I did when I was eating three meals a day, because we can live on cream and sugar for a long time. But, it is not good that we do this through our coffee, for our health's sake. I felt better eating one meal every two days, or 48 hours, with nothing between.

I also tried eating one meal every 72 hours, due to the fact that He had told me that if I ate one meal every three days, I would never be sick, and I thought I would try it, before teaching it. So, I did for a few months and I felt better than I felt when I was eating one meal every 48 hours. And, I can bear witness that I did not have the symptoms of illness at any time. My whole body felt light and my head was clear. I could almost hear insects crawling (smile).

IT IS NOT so much what you eat when you begin eating one meal everyday, or every two or three days, it is just that you do not eat foods that are against your health. I have described in this article, time and again that which He pointed out to me. But most people like us to eat the inexpensive food, because we do not have the finance to buy expensive foods that rich millionaires eat. So, He prescribed for us, dry navy beans, bread and milk.

The bread should be cooked thoroughly done, or either toasted, in order to cook it through. It should be made and risen by yeast. And, He Did Prescribe cooking this bread two or three times, if we would take time and do so. He said it was better for us.

No corn bread at all! He Said that it was too hard for our stomachs to digest. Corn was not made for us to turn it into meal to eat. It was made for live stock and cattle, and not for human consumption. The only corn that we eat, is that in the milk stage.

Eat butter, milk and fresh vegetables — but not your

old favorite collard greens, cabbage sprouts, turnip salads, mustard salads, beet top salads, kale, etc...

YOUR BEST vegetables are: cauliflower, cabbages (not the green cabbages). If you love turnips, eat the roots, not the salad. Some other vegetables we eat are as follows: brussel sprouts, asparagus, eggplant, okra, squash and rhubarb.

There are some asking about eating sardines. They are only for us to eat if we travel and cannot get other foods. But, please do not buy them, unless they are fresh where you can clean them, and not packed already. There are some packed that are clean, but they are a little expensive. They are called Portuguese sardines.

There are other herbs that we can eat that are not mentioned here. But, please, whenever you decide on eating something that is not in this book, write me, because there are some that are not good, on the market, for you and me.

Eating once every other day, the right foods, will get you the best of health and long life, as Allah has Taught me.

CHAPTER ELEVEN

THE KEY TO BETTER HEALTH

There is no question. If we eat right, we live. If we eat the wrong foods, it shortens our lives.

Some of us actually wish that we could live a thousand years, but be happy if you scale a hundred. The fact about it is you will not want to live too long (into the thousands of years). You will have nothing to attract you. You will have probably learned everything on the earth, and will have no place to go for attraction. Since you are on the earth, you cannot live elsewhere.

One meal a day and nothing between that one meal will get you a longer life, that is if you eat the proper food. We make ourselves sick. Do not think that sickness is something that just comes by itself, regardless to how we live. It is the way we live that makes us sick. I have experienced these things. If we do not eat the right foods to live, and do not eat it at the time that we should eat it, and eat before it is time; we will not live long.

Stay away from poison foods, such as pig (swine flesh). Do not eat it. Do not even touch its carcass. No swine flesh eater shall see the Hereafter; for in the Hereafter, there will be no pigs on the earth. They will be killed off. The swine was not made for Black People. It was made only for the white race. And, the white race teaches everybody to eat it, because it is a Divinely prohibited flesh; and they break all the Laws of God, because they are not supposed to obey the Laws of God. They have their own law, because they are the gods of this world. If they would follow and obey the Law of our God, they would be Muslims like us.

Eat one meal a day, and do not try to eat everything edible in that one meal. There is enough good food for you and me, for us to never eat other than good food. Eat to live.

CHAPTER TWELVE

DO NOT EAT BETWEEN MEALS

Eat one good meal of food a day for good health. One meal a day or every two days could spell the end of much medicine, doctor bills, and the building of hospitals if we would eat the proper food and eat it only when it is necessary to eat it.

There are a lot of people who think their appetite is their God; but we, by nature, have been made to control ourselves if we want to. I have much self-experience in the way of eating. I am often experimenting as I teach you, so that I will know what happens if you go contrary to the teachings of "How To Eat To Live." Eat one meal a day and eat the proper food in that meal, and do not be eating between meals (a little of this and a little of that). I repeat, you will not be sick (only once in a great long time).

Every meal that we put in our bodies has some poison in it. And, some of our food, as I have said in this book, takes 36 hours to digest. If we do not wait until our previous meal has been digested we add a new meal to the previous meal we have new poison, in its full strength, to aid the dying poison of the previous meal or to help it revive in strength; and we will continue to be sick.

This I have experienced. I suffered sickness a lot of times through experimenting, so that you will not come and give me the wrong answer to the teachings of "How To Eat To Live." I have self-experimented. I will know whether you are telling me the truth or not. But, I will put my life on it; that if you make a habit of eating one meal every day or every two days and of eating the right food, you will not be sick (only one day out of a year or out of every two years); and some of the complaints that you have now will completely disappear.

By eating one meal a day, some chronic diseases will vanish in a few years as they fail to get the poison that will keep them alive. Sometimes, they vanish within a few months, if you eat the right foods and eat only one meal a day or every two days. Try it for your-selves.

CHAPTER THIRTEEN

FASTING, EATING RIGHT FOODS, KEYS TO LONG LIFE

Eat Only One Meal A Day

Fasting is a greater cure of our ills—both mentally and physically—than all of the drugs of the earth combined into one bottle or into a billion bottles. Allah (God) in the Person of Master Fard Muhammad, has taught me that fasting and the right kind of food are the cures to our ills. He has told me there is no cure in drugs and medicine. And this, the world is now learning. We can take medicine all of our lives until it kills us, but we are still ailing with the same old diseases.

The bad food and drinks we are putting into our bodies keep us a victim to illness. There are not too many nice doctors who will tell you that drugs are not good for you, because they paid for their learning and want to keep practicing.

But "How to Eat to Live" is what we want to know, and have wanted to know all of our lives. Every man or woman wants to know how he (or she) can prolong his (or her) life.

Nature teaches us to stay here in this life as long as we can. Nature has never taught anyone that he should leave this life and find another one somewhere else, because we only have one life. If this life is destroyed, we would have a hard time trying to get more life; it is impossible. So, try to keep this life you have as long as possible. Go when you cannot stay here any longer.

ALLAH TAUGHT ME that one meal a day would keep us here for a long time; we would live over 100 years. And eating one meal every two days would lengthen our lives just that much longer. He told me you would never be sick, eating one meal every three days. The fact that fasting is the cure to 90 per cent of our ills is known by the medical scientists. But, they do not teach you that.

They know that tobacco, hard whiskey and alcohol are not good for you and will shorten your life and kill you. But most of them are too weak themselves to stop drinking or smoking or chewing tobacco. So they do not teach you that tobacco and alcoholic drinks—made into what is known as whiskey, beer and wine—are not good for you, although they know it to be true.

They will say, "Yes, it is good for you if you are temperate." But, they know that once you get started on that stuff, it is such an enemy that it just takes you into its power, and it is almost like trying to break an iron chain to get away from the habit. So do not use tobacco in any form and you will live a few years longer.

Fast once a month for three days or four days—or for whatever length of time you are able to go without food without harming yourself—and you will feel good. Did you not know that if you would stop eating pig and the food that you should not eat; stop eating three and four times a day and stop drinking whiskey, beer and wine, you would save much in the way of money?

In prolonging your life by abstaining from the pig, alcoholic drinks and tobacco, you, also, will be adding money to your savings of hundreds and thousands of dollars. You will be depriving those pig raisers and tobacco growers and alcoholic distilleries of millions of dollars that they rob you of which hasten you to your grave.

YOU COULD STOP the tobacco growers from growing that stinking weed, by turning away from the use of it. And you could stop the pig raising by not eat-ing the stinking hog. These things are death to your children in their early ages. And, they even affect the reproductive organs of people in the early ages, as well as affect the heart, the lungs, and your sharpness in thinking. And, after all of this, you die a victim of poison and commercialization. Learn to eat to live.

CHAPTER FOURTEEN

FASTING

There is so much food of various kinds in the earth for us to eat we could hardly mention by names.

We are the wisest of all life on the earth and in the heavens above the earth. Almighty God, Allah, in the Person of Master Fard Muhammad, to Whom Praise is due forever, has taught me. We must have regularity in everything we do.

SINCE THE earth is full of food, this does not mean we should try to eat the food all day long. We should eat one meal a day and when we eat this one meal, be sure it is of the best food for our bodies to digest and to keep us alive without our lives being agitated by enemies from the food and drinks we put in our bodies.

We have to safeguard our health against the enemies of our health by eating one meal a day. This gives an enemy (germ) that may be in our food time to die — to be completely dead at the end of twenty-four hours.

IF WE KEEP adding more food, it gives the germ strength and working power to destroy the very delicate and perfect machinery of our bodies. By nature, we are made of the best. And, we have to continue to give our bodies the best and in a moderate way.

Fasting is one of the greatest "doctors" we have. Fasting is prescribed for us in the Holy Qur-an and in the Bible. The Bible does not teach us as much of how good fasting is health-wise, as the Holy Qur-an does.

THE BIBLE'S teaching on fasting is mostly spiritual purposes. On one occasion, we find where Moses fasted for the cure of his sister, Miriam, who had contracted leprosy because of speaking carelessly of Moses. Her brother (Moses) then had to seek a cure from God for her.

But fasting, as Allah prescribed for us, is to prolong our lives with better health by eating the right food and not eating too frequently.

FASTING DOES much for us. A three-day fast will tell the story—you feel better; your body begins to feel lighter and not weighty as it felt when it was filled with food; your thinking is clearer.

Let us fast as often as we feel that we have not a desire for food. If you do not desire food, do not eat it. Eat when you are very hungry (of course, this does not apply to the sick, because the sick are exempt from fasting).

WHEN YOU fast, it will advance you spiritually. The Holy Qur-an teaches us that Allah has a mighty reward for the believing men and the believing women, and the fasting men and the fasting women. This does not mean that we can do nothing but fast and still do many other evil things and be rewarded with good rewards.

When fasting is practiced for good, good results will follow. But, if we fast, as the Bible mentions in Isiah, just for debate, our fast is no good. The Bible teaches that the facts of people who go out and tell others that "I had a dream" and then call dreams, visions, are not accepted.

SOME PEOPLE tell stories about something they accomplish on the fast that they did not accomplish. The Bible answers such a person in these words: If you dream a dream, tell a dream and do not try to tell a dream for a vision from the Lord, when you did not get such a vision.

We must remember that we cannot be "holier than thou," unless we are really holy. So, let us say of ourselves what we really are and not what we are not because it is good in the eye sight of God for us to speak the truth.

FAST! It cleans the impurities out of the blood and causes the body to eliminate the poison stored in it from previous meals — sometimes from previous meals of many years, as the folds in our intestines can carry particles of food for a long time, and holds strength enough in them to keep us alive for two months. Our bodies store food in the folds of the intestines and in the blood stream.

After a fast of three days — and from that to nine days — these particles of food and poison that have accumulated will be eliminated. The blood is being cleansed of its impurities because the impurities have nothing to keep them in power to live; therefore, they die and leave the person happy and enjoying the results of a healthy body — which is the greatest enjoyment we can have.

WE ARE TAUGHT...and all religions teach fasting...so that includes us too. Of course, as long as we are in the Presence of God, we do not have to fast. But, we are not always in His Presence. In the Hereafter when all people will receive rewards of goodness who see the Hereafter, there will be no fasting.

WE,THE RIGHTEOUS, must fast as long as we are present and among the unrighteous. So, fasting is prescribed for us as well as those (people) before us. Let us take a look at the verse in the Holy Qur'an 2:183 translated by Maulana Muhammad Ali (copyright — 1963): "O you who believe, fasting is prescribed for you, as it was prescribed for those before you, so that you may guard against evil." Here it tells us why fasting is prescribed for us. It guards us against doing evil. Read the footnote of Maulana Muhammad Ali's translation of this chapter for footnote. No. 225.

WE HERE (Elijah Muhammad and his Followers)...I prescribe for you the month of December to fast in — if you are able to take the fast — instead of the regular month that travels through the year, called Ramadan by the Muslims; the month in which they say Muhammad received the Holy Qur'an.

WHY DID I prescribe for you the month of December? It is because it was in this month that you used to worship a dead prophet by the name of Jesus. And, it was the month that you wasted your money and wealth to worship the 25th day of this month, December, as the Christians do. The Christians know that it is not the birthday of Jesus; for they do not know the birthday of Jesus. No one knows it, because being persecuted by the Jews, Joseph and Mary feared the death of not only their newborn baby that they were bringing to birth, but even feared for their own lives for committing the act out of wedlock. They feared Herod and his army and the religious set of the Jews condemning them to be punished with death. But, they were not to be killed for they were for a sign of the Black Man in America, according to the Holy Qur-an. See Holy Qur-an, Chapter 4:171.

While the Christians have deceived you in worshipping the birthday of Nimrod who was born the 25th day of that month, no man knows the day Jesus was born, but they (Joseph and Mary) themselves. This is a sign right there; no man of the evil world was to know when the spiritual birth of Muhammad was to take place. And, most surely they do not know. So, do not fast as the other religious people fast, for they have different objects and ways in which they fast, which are against the meaningful fasts that we take.

FASTING takes away evil desires. Fasting takes from us filthy desires. Fasting takes from us the desire to do evil against self and our brothers and sisters. We are created of the material of goodness. Therefore, good belongs to us...and it should not be hard for us to turn to our own selves in which we were created...good.

WE are approaching the month of December, in which we usually abstain from eating in the daylight hours, as the Orthodox Muslims do, the ninth (9th) month of their calendar, the month of Ramadan.

I set up this for you and me, to try to drive out of us the old white slavemaster's worship of a false birthday (December 25th) of Jesus.

ALLAH (God) Who Came in the Person of Master Fard Muhammad, to Whom Praises are due forever, Taught me, that Jesus was not even born during the entire month of December.

THE scholars agree, that according to their history, Jesus could not have been born in December.

ALLAH (God) Taught me that Jesus was born between the first and the second week in September, instead of December. But, no one knew the day of Jesus' birth except Joseph and Mary.

BECAUSE of the Jews' hot prosecution against the birth of Jesus, the exact day of his birth was kept a secret, from the public. So, to break my people up from the worship of a false birthday of Jesus, we turned to abstaining from eating in the daylight hours during the month of December. This is, in no way, a FAST!

WHEN we abstain from food for so short a time as for early morning until after sundown and darkness begins to appear — we cannot call this a FAST, for we are eating the same way that we have always been eating (one meal in that day). IT is no FAST to me and to my followers to eat a meal after Sunday. We cannot call it a FAST!

A FAST should be from two (2) to three (3) days without eating food. If we are seeking spiritual advancement, we should fast for three days.

IN the case of the Orthodox Muslims worshipping Ramadan by not eating until after sunset, and darkness approaches (they can eat all night long if they want to, until the next morning at dawn) — they call this a FAST!

THEY say that they do this in the Month of Ramadan because Ramadan is the month in which the Holy Quran was revealed to Muhammad.

BUT, the way that I understand scripture, it

teaches us that Muhammad received the Holy Qur-an over a period of twenty-three (23) years.

MUHAMMAD did not receive the Holy Qur-an in one night or in one day. And, if he received the whole Holy Qur'an in the month of Ramadan, WHY FAST in that month?

IF we are given what we want (Holy Qur'an) in that month, without FASTING, I cannot understand why we should FAST in the month of Ramadan, for the first revelation of the Holy Qur'an was already given in that month, without FASTING.

IT would look more proper for us to be rejoicing over the great salvation (Holy Qur'an) that Allah (God) sent to us, in the month of Ramadan.

If you can convince me it is necessary to Fast in the month of Ramadan because of Muhammad receiving the Holy Quran, or the first revelation of the Holy Qur-an, then I will go along with it. However since the Qur-an was received over a period of years, I am very much baffled in trying to understand why we should FAST in the month of Ramadan.

WE should be rejoicing because of receiving the Holy Qur'an and we should teach others to rejoice throughout the month of Ramadan, if it is because the Holy Qur'an was revealed in that month.

OF COURSE, this is the Arab way, in their religious belief, that they should FAST. But I do say that it is not necessary to FAST to get something that you have already received.

WE should all thank Allah and be grateful to Allah (God) for Giving us the truth, or the Great

Revelation (Holy Qur'an), that will guide us into a clearer truth than we have had in the past.

SO, I am not asking my followers to FAST in the month of December because of the birth of a prophet (Jesus) nor do we want to worship his birth or worship because some great revelation was sent down to another prophet. No, it is just to keep my followers from worshipping falsehood, instead of truth, and to prevent them from spending their money in the falsehood, instead of truth, and to prevent them from spending their money in the falsehood of Santa Claus.

There are so many untruths that the people of untruth (white race) have mislead us in. We must come out of untruth, we must come out of falsehood.

I do know that FASTING is good. I have tried FASTING for many years myself. I do know that FASTING is good for our health and FASTING is good for our spiritual advancement.

IT is actually good for us to take a FAST and abstain from eating food for a period of days.

BUT, you are not actually FASTING when you are going to eat everyday, regardless to what time you may set for the meal. If you eat within twenty - four (24) hours, you cannot really consider it as a FAST.

AND, so I say to my followers, WE ARE NOT FASTING (in December) we are just abstaining from taking a part with false worship. We abstain from eating meat throughout the month of Ramadan— the month of December.

IT is good for us to abstain from eating meat, for we should not eat meat at all. Meat is not good for our health nor for our body.

ACTUALLY by nature, we are not made to live off meat.

ALLAH, (God) Who Came in the Person of Master Fard Muhammad, to Whom Praises are due forever, Taught me, that no meat is good for us, except the little young pigeon (squab) that has never flown from its nest. But, we eat meat.

BEEF—coarse meat, such as beef—we should not wear out our stomach trying to digest this coarse meat. We should not eat any meat—not even lamb.

FISH—we can eat fish. Fish is raised under a different atmosphere. Fish is from a different world of life. Fish is born and fish lives, in the water of life. Fish is good for us.

BIRDS—ALLAH (God) Taught me that no bird is good for us to eat, and if you watch the nature of a bird, you will also agree that the bird is not fit to eat.

BUT, following a people who the Holy Qur'an describes as 'eating like a beast' (white race)—they eat anything that they want to eat and they do not care concerning the harm that it is doing to their life. It is hard to live a hundred (100) years eating the way the white race eats—not to think of being able to live from 200 to 900 years like Noah and Methuselah lived.

ALLAH (God) Who Came in the Person of Master Fard Muhammad, to Whom Praises are due forever, Taught me, that the people of the planet Mars lives 1,200 of our earth years.

I do not know what they eat of their planet life, as Allah (God) did not Teach me what they eat. And I did not ask Him in the first place.

THE PEOPLE of MARS eat what their planet produces for them to eat, as the planet produced the people of Mars and it produces the food that they eat. I do not know what the planet produces, other than the people of Mars.

IF I could fly to Mars, I do not know whether I could say, "Prepare, fish, lamb or chicken," and have it prepared for me.

FAST—for 3 days—FAST for 3X3 days, FAST for 9 days or FAST for 27 days. FASTING is good for us. It gives our blood time to cleanse itself, and in so doing it makes us think clearer.

IF you make a habit of FASTING—you are not going to get sick. Abstain from eating, if you are eating the right kind of food, you can FAST but when you eat again, you poison your body.

STAY AWAY from that which is not good for us.

ABSTAINING FROM FOOD, FROM THE RISING OF THE SUN, UNTIL THE SUN SETS—THIS IS NOT FASTING.

CHAPTER FIFTEEN

FASTING IS PRESCRIBED

Eat good food which has been prescribed in this book. Do not eat over one meal a day.

Dry beans (navy beans) and whole bread are good for us. We do not have to go around looking for all kinds of foods. Just one common kind will do. Give the body some time to rest.

FASTING is a great act upon true Believers of the true religion of God (Islam). This also helps prolong our lives.

It is prescribed for us in the Law of the religion of Islam (Holy Qur-an). All Muslims who respect fasting should take the fast of Ramadan. We are not taking the month of Ramadan as prescribed in the Holy Qur-an. We take the Christians' month (December, the twelfth month), instead of the ninth month.

This month I prescribe for you to fast (the twelfth month of the Christian year) for the purpose of getting you away from the false teaching of the Jesus' Birth on the 25th of December. God Has Taught Me that he was born between the first and the second week of September and not December.

This day, (the 25th of December) He taught Me was the birth date of that demon Nimrod, who was born in the Seventeenth century of Moses' era before the birth of Jesus.

He was so wicked that the Scholars and Scientists of Scripture of the Prophets do not like to teach you of this history of Nimrod. And, if it was the birthdate of that righteous Prophet Jesus, you most certainly in your celebration of the 25th of December have not been showing a clean and holy celebration of a right-eous person with your drunkenness and your gambling. Your everything but right is committed on the 25th day of December in celebrating the birth of a righteous man. But, you are not doing so for righteousness, you are celebrating the birth date of an evil person and the white Christians will send you all the whiskey and beer and wine and swine that you want to eat and drink on that day.

RAMADAN is the ninth month of the Arab year (which is also twelve months and not nine months). The Holy Qur-an teaches that twelve months have always been a year with God. We are not able to satisfy the astro-nomists if we do not have a twelve month year, for it takes the earth 12 months to make its complete circuit around the sun and this is why we call it one year (af-ter its completion of this circuit made by the earth as an average distance of 93 million miles).

Ramadan, the Holy Qur-an teaches us, is the month that the Holy Qur-an was revealed to Mu-hammad. And they worship the month by abstaining from eating and drinking during the day time from sun up to sun down or before the sun rises until after she sets in the Western skies.

Then, after dark, we can eat and drink until the sun rises again the next day. The significances of this Arabic fasting in Ramadan is that the spiritual dark-ness of Yakub's made man (the white race); eating and drinking, sport and play was the order of the white world, until the day break of Truth coming in the first of the seven thousand years after the six thousand years of spiritual darkness and evil of the white man's world.

WE ARE living now in the bright spiritual world of Allah, the Great Mahdi in the Person of Master Fard Muhammad, to Whom Praise is due forever, therefore we are not the children of darkness, but the children of light and truth.

Actually, Divinely, there is no fast set for the children of the light of God and their fasting ceases. But, until we have accomplished our work of perfection of self and separation of us from the spiritual darkness of Yakub's made man and teachings, we fast to get out of it and take a month that we used to worship as being the month in which the birth of Jesus came about.

There is no such thing that we should worship any white people's holidays. All that they worship are their days and not the slaves (the Black peoples) days.

There is not one that we should worship. The past Thanksgiving Day that you were celebrating — what you have to thank God and man for that last Thursday of November ? Surely you should thank God for allowing you to live to see that day, but this was the man's day (Yakub's made man).

The Black Man should not take any part in any white people's holidays not even to Sunday. These are not our days. Please remember this.

I WILL take you further into this knowledge if you write me, as space here in our book is limited.

The Muslims, as I foresaid, do not eat nor drink from before sunrise until after she (the sun) has set. If you take it (the fast of Ramadan) with them, you are doing the right thing, until this evil world has vanished.

BECAUSE OF the fascination of food to the eye, the smell of food, and the imaginary taste of food, we follow our eyes and our tastes to our graves, by eating the wrong food too often.

CHAPTER SIXTEEN

ONE MEAL A DAY

The way we eat is one of the greatest problems that we have. It is the base of our illness.

ALLAH (GOD), in the Person of Master Fard Muhammad, to Whom praise is due forever, Says that what we eat keeps us here and what we eat takes us away. This is a very logical way of saying it.

He also Said that nature has not set a certain time for anyone to die. We live as long as we are able to keep living, according to what we eat and drink. This is universally known by the wise.

There are so many complaints about the poison that is now in our food and in our drink, which is placed there deliberately by the enemy, according to those who have the knowledge to detect the poison that is present in our food and drinks. The enemy has complete access to the food and drink (water).

A COUPLE OF years ago, in Phoenix, Arizona, after the burning and wreckage of our Mosque in New York, there were a few shots made at my house in Phoenix. One white man in Phoenix used these words: "Do not shoot him; get him in his water."

People of that type cannot be trusted. They are very dangerous, especially when they have access to your food and water. There was nothing to have caused this act of evil against me and my property, but evil is already there in the very nature of the people. They only want an excuse to practice that which they are made to do, by nature (evil and murdering the poor black man).

The slave master's continuous desire to murder his loyal free slaves, is a proof that there is no love, mercy, and peace in the hearts of these people, as God Has Taught me.

Why keep looking for that which by nature is not there? Separation is the only way out of it.

STAND UP for self and let us do something for self and quit laying yourselves down to be nursed by others. Eat to live; one meal a day and not three meals a day.

TYPE OF FOODS TO EAT

CHAPTER SEVENTEEN

MEAT IS AGAINST LIFE

We have found that eating one meal every 24 hours of the best food we possibly can find — which contains not so much poison for the body to assimilate — with long intervals between meals is better for our health, and also will prolong our lives.

IF WE EAT twice a week, this would make us to live twice as long as we would live by eating once every day or every other day.

Our bodies are made of the earth and contain a little of every matter of the earth's chemicals, stone, gold and silver.

TO EAT MEAT is against our life and shortens the span of our life. We eat meat because it is a habit from childhood. But if we eat meat only once a day or every other day or twice a week, it will not be so hard on our digestion. It won't shorten our lives as fast as eating it two and three times a day. Beef is hard on our digestion. It is too tough and coarse.

Lamb is not a salvation meat for us. It also is hard to digest, though it is a little better than beef. Lamb does not attract germs as beef, because sheep will not eat certain types of vegetation that cows will eat. Sheep are very careful about what they eat—like horses.

THE MILK OF these animals is all right to drink if their health is safeguarded against diseases, especially tuberculosis.

Fresh fruit and fresh edible vegetables and good pure wheat bread, pure milk and butter are the best food for man.

A LOT OF SWEETS is not at all good for man. There is enough sugar in fruits, vegetables and bread for us (notably sugars from sweets, wheat, cane and beets), without our need to prepare and refine any to such a sweet degree that it causes sickness in the body of man, i.e., diabetes and other such ailments caused by too much sugar in the body.

But whatever you eat, by taking long intervals between the meals (such as days), the effect will have time to destroy itself, if not added to by new meals.

OF COURSE, SUCH things as swine flesh, which creates a live poison in our body—often called "pork-worms" which also produces larger worms called "tapeworms,"—and destroys human life, from our early childhood to a short span of 50 to 75 years (which should just be the beginning of life).

Do not be a meat consumer. Be a vegetarian. This is the best menu for our health.

A MAN 200 or 300 years old is not an old man, if he has eaten the right food and taken it once every two or three days. A man can live 1,000 years if he eats the right food twice a week.

This is the teaching of Master Fard Muhammad (God in Person) to me. Follow it and you will lengthen your life.

CHAPTER EIGHTEEN

EAT THE BEST OF THINGS

MAN AND MANKIND'S best scientists have studied for centuries and for thousands of years on what one should eat to live. Now this great knowledge comes from the Mouth of The Wisest of them all to Guide, Teach, and Train the victim (you and me) of the world. We should be thankful for the attention, sympathy, mercy, and forgiveness from such a Great One as God in the Person of Master Fard Muhammad.

THE GREAT STRESS of 'How To Eat To Live' is made upon one meal a day. There is no doubt that one meal once every 24 hours of the right food will lengthen our lives and produce better enjoyment of our lives. Some of the various kinds of foods, of which you have no knowledge of its reaction in the stomach before you eat it, shortens the life. Never say that you will eat anything. Say that you will eat the best of things.

THE GREAT POISON dishes that are set before you and that you are dining off of daily, and that some of you eat three and four times a day are:

Number 1: The filthy hog meat

Number 2: Beans that cattle should eat. And, that is what they are made for and not for human consumption Lima beans, butter beans, field peas, black eyed peas, and even soy beans are not good for anything but for shortening your life.

CORN BREAD, half-done flour bread, and sweet potatoes, all shortens your life. The sweet potato is

not good for any human to take as a food. White potatoes do very well but they produce too much starch
which would add fat, and too much fat shortens the
life. This, I want you fat readers to remember; that
your rolly, rosey fat does not mean long life. It means
short life to you. Stay away from eating corn bread. It
is too rough for the stomach. It wears out the stomach
like sand grinds away a delicate rug on your floor.

THERE ARE MANY vegetables that we could eat
if the right kinds are pointed out to you. Stay away
from collard greens and cabbage sprouts, such food is
horse and cattle food. Oh, I know what you may say,
my Black Brothers and Sisters, "I have been eating it
all my life and my grandmother and father ate it and
they lived 65, 75, or 80 years." That is no time to live!
You need to live not under 100 years, and from that to
one thousand years. But, your life depends on what you
eat. What you eat keeps you here and what you eat
takes you away.

CHAPTER NINETEEN
TRY AND EAT FRESH FOODS

EAT ONE MEAL at the end of every 24 hours and nothing between, if you are not sick. If you are sick, that is different. Sickness takes away strength. Therefore, you have to eat something like food to replace it. But, if you are well and want to stay well, eat only one meal a day. And, eat good food. Regardless to the variety of foods that which is best for you to eat, and eat it. Do not try eating all the different types of foods, lest you will be found dead one morning in your bed. And, try and eat fresh foods and not stale foods. Cook it done, and not half done. Just done and that is all, not too done that all of the taste is out of it through cooking.

STAY AWAY FROM eating a lot of meats and do not eat too much fish that is weighing from 20 to 50 pounds. You should eat fish weighing a half pound to ten pounds. And, be sure not to eat the scavenger fish that lives off of filth. Do not eat a fish that sucks its food, but eat one that swallows its food whole. Do not eat fish that look like animals, with heads like animals, nor forefronts built like an animal. Do not eat such fish as eel, which should not really be referred to as a fish, but as a water snake. And, never eat slimy oysters, lobsters, crabs, clams, shrimps and snails.

FOR YOUR OWN good health, and for the sake of the Law of Allah (God), do not think of going near a piece of carcass of the swine (hog). Do not burn your hearts and brains up with alcoholic liquids.

DO NOT EAT field peas, black eyed peas, brown

peas, yellow peas nor red peas. Do not eat the great big lima beans nor the little lima beans. The only kidney-like bean should you eat, as Allah (God) Taught me, is the navy bean. There are the white ones and the red ones. You may eat them. Do not eat too many green greens. They are not good for you. Especially the collard greens and the cabbage sprouts. Do not eat them. There are plenty of herbs and vegetables that you can eat other than these. But, seek mostly the white ones, such as white-head cabbage and white cauliflower.

YOU MAY SAY this type of food, that I am mentioning to you, is high. But life is high and to keep it, you had better eat the things that will maintain that high life. You and I live only but once. Eat the good things of life and think good things. Do not fill the brains up with evil thoughts. Think good things and then you will be good. I hope that you will take this for your own sake. How to eat to live.

CHAPTER TWENTY

SIMPLE FOODS ARE BEST

Allah (God) Who Came in the Person of Master Fard Muhammad, to Whom Praises are due forever, taught us HOW TO EAT TO LIVE without being tormented with sickness and disease.

DO NOT LOOK at me when you see me sick. This suffering is what I have to go through with to prove myself worthy of being the Last Messenger of Allah. I am afflicted with everything that you are afflicted with. According to the Bible, Isaiah, Chapter 53, 'In all of your afflictions he was afflicted.' Allah (God) Wants To Show you in the example that He makes of me, that I have suffered the same afflictions that you have, so that you will not have this as an excuse for your disbelieving. You cannot claim that I did not suffer the same things that you suffered, that God Would Not Have Found me to be the good Messenger.

I suffer sickness with you. I suffered imprisonment with you. I suffered the deprivation of family as you have. Show me what you have suffered, that I have not suffered. It is necessary for the Last Messenger to suffer a taste of what all of the prophets before him suffered. Therefore, the Last Messenger is called the fulfillment of the prophets. He fulfills the same history of the former prophets...except death. He is not to be murdered...God Will Not Suffer that.

IT IS hard to get pure, good, healthy food for those who desire it. The enemy, the devil has poisoned everything. He has poisoned the Bible and the food that we eat. But, do the best that you can until he has been removed. The devil seeks to remove you with himself. Allah (God) Has Power over all things.

WHEN I was in Phoenix, Arizona, a few years ago, before I arrived some one had fired shots at my house. Another devil said, "Do not shoot him, get him in his water." What had I done to be shot or poisoned for? That shows that they are the murderers of the prophets of old, and that Allah (God) Should Take revenge on this generation for the righteous that they killed before.

WE look too much at the fancy and the artificial foods that the enemy made and accepted for himself. He eats just the opposite things from that which the righteous eat.

SIMPLE foods are the best. The Bible warns us to beware of the dainty foods of the enemy. Meats are not good for us, but we eat meat.

But, do not eat the swine flesh. We should not eat any stale meat. What I mean is that we should not eat food that is ready to become rotten — poison. When food smells like it is spoiled, we should not eat it.

THIS is why I ask you all the day long to help me and my followers to purchase farms, although they are hard to get. When they look up and see the poor Black once-slave wanting to buy the farm, they raise the price and keep the Black once-slave at his mercy to eat whatever food the enemy, white slave master prepares for him.

Allah, (God), Master Fard Muhammad, to Whom Praises are due forever, Has Taught us that the white man is the devil and you will agree with me one of these days...that he is just that...the devil. He cannot help himself. He is doing what he was made to do. Neither can I help doing what I was made to do—to preach the truth while the devil preaches falsehood.

SIMPLE navy beans is one of the best foods that we can eat. You do not have to strain the beans to eat them. Straining the beans is a real habit that we took up years ago. But, they are better if you eat them in their hull (skin).

DO NOT put a lot of spices, or what you call seasoning, in such good food. Do not do this. You ruin your food. The value of the bean is taken away by your putting so much seasoning in them. Just put the beans on and cook them until they are done. Let the beans stay in its jacket. Of course I see them crush the beans, and since the cooks and the eaters like it like that, I go along with them. But I like it better when you just cook them right in the jacket.

I FEEL like I could eat a bowl full of beans right now while I am talking about it. You can eat that bean seven (7) days a week. It is very appealing to the appetite.

WE SHOULD have a great field of hundreds and thousands of acres of beans to feed our people. It is a very cheap and a very healthy food for us. We should buy canning factories for ourselves and can beans. If you want meat in them, just put a taste of chicken in them to give them the flavor of meat. Or put a little piece of lamb or beef, but not enough to make it part of the contents of the can of beans. Just put enough in them for flavoring. Or you can take the essence of lamb or beef and pour a little of it in the beans. You will have to put a little piece of the flesh of the lamb or beef in the beans if you want meat because the tallow of beef does not taste good.

THE Bible and the Holy Qur-an both forbid us from eating the fat of anything, regardless of what life it is—fowl or animal.

LET US take a look at the bread of the Southern Black People. They were born eating corn bread. It was the first bread that they ate. It is a very shame-ful thing to do to give an infant rough corn bread to put in his tender little milk-stomach. This is why so many of them have stomachs with ulcers and cancers.

FEED your children good navy beans (small size pink, red or white) there are many that are good for you and me. Take those freshly cooked and iced cakes off of the table. They are not good for you and me, unless they were cooked two times. Cook plain cakes and do not ice them over with bought essence to make icing with. If you want icing, make your own icing with sugar or eggs.

EAT THAT which is good. I am not saying that there are not good foods. I am just telling you that the simple foods are the best.

IF you just love corn bread because our fathers were brought up by the white slave-master to eat all of these rough foods, Allah (God) Master Fard Muhammad, to Whom Praises are due forever Taught me that we should cook it two or three times. Each time add a little flour to it and let it set for RISING. Put yeast in and let it rise and rise and rise.

Allah (God) in the Person of Master Fard Muhammad, to Whom Praises are due forever, Taught me that the food that we eat keeps us here and what we eat takes us away from here. I thank Him for Teaching me what was good for me to eat and what was bad for me to eat.

WE the Black People need to plant wheat and to raise all of the wheat flour that we can raise. We need to have great farms of pigeon-birds and eat only the ones who are too young to leave their nest. We call them squab. Allah (God) Said to me that this young bird is the only one that is fit for us to eat and do not eat Him after he flies from the nest. Chicken is not good for us to eat although we eat it. As you know the chicken is as filthy as the swine or the dog. He is a very filthy fowl and if you want to eat him, do not let him get away from you and stray out of the coop. Keep him closed up and feed him what you want him to eat. Never let him get out and eat bugs and worms. Feed him the things you know are good and pure. When he is fat you can kill and eat him. This still does not mean that he is too good for us. You have to study up on ways to protect his eating, for he will turn right around and eat his own droppings.

SO, for the habitual meat-eater, it is hard to get the right food, especially if you want meat. It is dangerous for your health to eat daintily prepared meals with all kinds of meat and all kinds of sugary bread prepared by someone's recipe.

STAY away from the foods and the styles of the Christians. Ninety-five per cent of the foods that the Christians eat are unfit for good health and long life.

THERE is much fruits and vegetables that are good for us, but I do not have space to take them all up with you. Many of these are not injurious to our health. There are some people who eat only fruits and vegetables. They are vegetarians and they live a long time—those who do not go after the wrong kind of vegetables and fruits.

DO NOT EAT such foods as collard greens. Do not eat black eyed peas, or brown black and many other peas. They are not good for your stomach. Feed them to the cattle. Do not eat baby or adult lima beans. Do not eat belly-busters. Allah (God) Taught me that no peas are good for you other than the ones that I have already announced to you.

HOW TO EAT TO LIVE—there are many of my little Black Brothers who are hungry for offers and for leadership and they commercialize on what you find me writing. They take my writings and put it into other aspects and add in, and out of it, and offer it up, for a sale price, because he does not want to do some-thing for self. He wants to take everything that he can and commercialize on it. He is a thief and a robber under the disguise of putting out the teachings of the Messenger. You know my way of putting the teachings out. If I charge for some literature it is because I want to get back what we put into it and put the profit to work to build a nation. But, you are selfish and this is why I do not give you any credit.

TAKE this that I give to the people directly, and do not add to it to try and make money. Allah (God) Has Already Promised you Money but do not try to make money out of His Word. There are people now who are trying to put some of their work, copied from my work, and with their own no-good additions to it.

LEAVE MY teachings as it is. No wonder the Jesus had to run the money-changers out of the Synagogue. They who were turning it into a market-place to sell their produces of this and that. You are doing the same.

You want to give little parties and dinners to commercialize on your place of teaching. They do not do that in their Holy Land. They do not take their prayer-house and turn it into a market.

WHEN a person is sick, he may have to eat two or three meals a day. The Holy Qur'an does not prescribe fasting for a person if he is sick. You cannot take fasts if you are sick. And you have to eat more than one or two meals a day until you are well again. But, Black Brother, if you have a pretty good hearty appetite do not do this and claim that you are sick when you eat that way.

HOW TO EAT TO LIVE. Eat only when necessary. when you are hungry and not before. Eat the right food. When you eat, fill up and eat until that is gone away and then fill up again.

LOOK at the camel. He fills his stomach with water then he goes a long time off of this one drink. Do not eat another fresh meal while the other is in the process of digesting, if you are well. If you are sick the complaint or the disease eats up the value of the food quickly, and you have to replenish it, so that you can continue to stay strong or rid yourself of the complaint or sickness, as the doctor will prescribe for you.

WHEN you are well again eat one meal and eat the right kind of food and you will live one hundred and forty (140) years, so Allah (God) Taught me. Eat one meal every twenty-four hours and eat good simple food. Remember to cook your food thoroughly before you eat it. This does not mean that you should cook your food into a waste, but just cook it so long as it is done and it is not half-done. Half cooked food will ruin your digestive system.

CHAPTER TWENTY ONE

DO NOT EAT SCAVENGERS

Eat the best food you can obtain. Never deprive yourself of good health, at the price of cheap food. Just remember, when you are feeding your stomach with cheap, poison foods trying to keep a dollar in your pocket, you are not saving a dollar in your pocket.

IT WILL only go to the hospital, the undertaker, and for the ever increasing drain on the families' savings in purchasing drug pacifications for the ill body from eating the wrong food.

There is not one of you who would not like to live a long, long time. That long time depends on what you eat and drink. So, eat and drink that which is good. Go to the farm and try raising your own food, or have collective farming. However, try seeking some of this earth that you can call your own; and, raise on it the necessities of life.

And, in this way, you may be able — if you can keep your lurking enemy from slipping poison into your good and innocent crops — to grow pure food. We cannot blame the white man for his evils, because by nature he was made like that. But, we can blame ourselves for accepting such evil.

I have received many questions in regard to meat, fish, and poultry that have not been mentioned. The main thing Allah, as well as the Holy Qur-an, reminds us of is that when it comes to meat and fish, Allah forbids us to eat the flesh of a swine and a fish weighing over 50 pounds (or even weighing 50 pounds).

SOME PEOPLE will not even eat fish at all. There are many fish that we can eat; some even weighing as little as one or one and a half pounds.

When eating fish, we should confine our fish - eating to those fish weighing between one and ten pounds. As I previously said on "HOW TO EAT TO LIVE," do not eat the scavengers of the sea such as oysters, crabs, clams, snails, shrimps, eels, and catfish.

The fish last mentioned (catfish) is a very filthy fish. He loves filth and is the pig of the water. Some people write in complaining about the fish that swim on their sides, but these fish can be eaten.

ALLAH HAS Taught me that chicken is not good to eat. They are quite filthy (in-as-much as they do not eat the cleanest of food), but we eat them.

We eat beef and lamb; but Allah also said that it is not so good for us. It is not a sin for us to eat it. It is not a sin for us to eat camels. But if we can find better food, we should not eat the above mentioned food. Many write and ask if they should eat meat at all. It is not a sin for you to eat meat, but it is a sin for you to eat the hog -meat.

If we want to prolong our lives, it is best that we do not eat meat or do not eat it so often. Beef is very coarse and many or our people do not eat it because of that. Horsemeat can also be eaten. It is cleaner than the average meat. But we should not eat it unless we are extremely hungry and have nothing else to eat because it is a domestic animal and is gentle and close to the home.

IT IS NOT A sin to eat even, rabbit. But since Allah said that the rabbit is so near kin to the house cat that they are relatives, we do not eat it. The rabbit, however, is cleaner than the house cat because he eats vegetables, roots, and herbs and he does not eat anything alive.

CHAPTER TWENTY TWO

ALWAYS PREPARE A GOOD MEAL

Since God Almighty has given us the truth—the spiritual truth—then He (Allah) must give us physical guidance to protect the life of the spiritual truth.

THERE ARE MANY varieties of food that the earth produces to which we can help ourselves if we want. But there is only a small amount of the variety of foods that we can eat in order to live and prosper.

The white race has produced all kinds of foods, but they are not all good for human consumption, in the way of enjoying good health and long life. Eating the wrong food can cause you to suffer much sickness.

The Bible has a very ignorant way of teaching us the proper foods. In the beginning of the creation of Adam, in Genesis, it says, every herb and all the fruits of the trees are good for you to eat. It is ignorant to believe such a thing as that. You try it (eating all of these things) and you will die.

The earth produces every kind of fruit for every kind of life on the earth. Whereas the monkey can live off nuts and bananas, and other animals thrive on such foods, just these foods will destroy us. Making our stomachs digest nuts will shorten our lives.

IF WE MAKE A habit of living off the flesh of their lives, it will shorten our lives. Our stomachs are not made by nature to digest flesh and yet continue to produce or prolong our lives, because the flesh wears away the stomach. The eating of the flesh of other creatures is not good for our flesh.

There are many varieties of sea flesh—fish as we call it—that we go to sea to capture for food. We should be careful not to eat every fish, because every fish is not good to eat. If a fish weighs 50 pounds, we should not eat it. God Almighty has taught me that it is too hard on your digestive system.

He (Allah) said to me that even eating peanuts, walnuts and all of the other types of nuts you find these people (white people) eating, will take away five years of your life. Just one meal of them destroys five years of your life.

Question the doctors on how the nuts react in the stomach against good health and the prolongation of life—they will bear witness.

THERE IS ONE flesh that the enemy has brought us to eat that is an abomination in the eyes of Allah (God); that is the flesh of the swine. You cannot even join onto your own people today if you are a swine eater.

White America will do its utmost to test you if you say you do not love the swine. This proves, beyond a shadow of a doubt, that the white race is an enemy to the law of Allah (God) and wishes to make everyone of us disobey the law of Allah (God).

What God said "thou shalt not do," they teach you to do. The white race has been an enemy of Allah (God) every since they were made. Therefore, their way of eating shortens life. Sometimes their life is less than half of a hundred years.

By eating this poison food three times a day, you cut off 2/3 (two-thirds) of your life. Always prepare yourself a good meal once a day, and do not eat any more until the next day at the same time, if you can. You will find a change in the way you feel and you will find that you can say to the doctor, I do not need you and your poison drugs.

WE CANNOT blame doctors for commercializing on us after they have studied for their profession, for it makes them anxious to benefit from their profession. The proper way to live is the way that nature and the guidance of Allah (God) teaches us to.

CHAPTER TWENTY THREE

COOKED FOOD IS BETTER

For good health and long life, God, in the Person of Master Fard Muhammad, taught me that we should eat one meal a day and it should be 24 hours from the last meal. If we eat one meal once every day at four o'clock or six o'clock (whatever is the best hour for your meal), then wait until that hour comes again before eating again.

TRY EATING one meal a day for yourself and you will tell me you feel much better than you did eating three times a day. A lot of little complaints or ailments will disappear.

You do not have to eat every menu that is pre-scribed by this civilization. If you do, you will be dead—and soon. This civilization is rapidly turning back to raw food and raw juices, but our God and Saviour Allah (God), in the Person of Master Fard Muhammad, taught me to cook our food and most of the doctors agree that cooked food is better.

THERE ARE many doctors who will not agree with you on drinking a lot of raw juices—not even a lot of raw grape juice, orange juice, or any kind of fresh juice. It is too much for our stomachs. The vitamins in it are good for us but there are other enemies in raw vegetables and fruit juices from the land where they were grown and from the insects that fed upon them.

When we eat raw vegetables as they come up from the earth and other roots and salads which are raw, we are not doing our stomachs good. Our stomachs were not made to digest these foods in their first raw stages. Therefore, I do not agree with anyone on eating too much raw food or drinking too much raw juice.

A LITTLE raw salad is good for us, if eaten along with cooked food—even if we eat it daily—but do not make meals of such raw salad.

We cannot follow the white man in his eating habits, because his habits are from the days of savagery in the hills and caves of Europe, where he ate all his food raw, because he did not have the knowledge of the use of fire to cook his food, as he does today. EAT TO LIVE AND NOT TO DIE.

CHAPTER TWENTY FOUR

NATURAL FOOD

We are often making suggestions of the various kinds of foods that the earth produces for us to eat.

SINCE the coming of the white race, they (white race) have set forth one of the greatest confusions of what foods the human family should eat, and today everything like food is eaten by the human family. Whether this food is good for human consumption or not, it is offered in the market for us to eat.

Naturally, all follow what the white race offers to us in the way of eating, clothes, shelters and money because of their given power to rule over us for a limited time (6,000 years). We have followed their dictation as to what we should accept and what we should reject almost to the letter for the past 6,000 years.

Now, a New Ruler and His way of civilization stands knocking on our door with His list of how to eat to live.

In the Creation of the earth, the Creator caused everything to grow in the earth that would be, or act as, the sustainer of our lives.

The natural food value of the vegetables that we go to the market and buy should not be destroyed with a lot of additions. They contain the vitamins and proteins nature put in them for us, if the experimenters and poisoners of food do not interfere.

Natural food will give to us natural health and beauty and prolong our lives, if the poison hand of the commercializer does not touch it.

None of us should suffer with sugar diabetes if we would eat natural food, because the sugar in natural food is not enough to poison our blood with sugar. It is the sugar that is manufactured by the commercializers on sweets that causes the dreadful disease of sugar diabetes.

All suffers from sugar diabetes should abstain from eating sugar after they learn they are suffers from diabetes and they should eat the natural food that Allah has placed in the earth for us, without the addition of sugar.

WE SHOULD cook the food the way we like it and season it with a little natural salt and natural pepper the way we like it.

It is sometimes hard to get natural salt. There are several salts on the market that the commercializers on food have put before us. The best salt is the natural salt or that which the Jewish people eat and season their food with. The Jews are old settlers of the white civilization and the first guides of the white race in the natural and commercial field of foods.

The Holy Qur-an teaches the Muslims that the food of both the followers of Moses (the Orthodox Jews) and the food of the Muslims is good for each, because the foods of the two people do not vary too much. There are some weak Muslims and there are some weak Orthodox Jews but they (Orthodox Jews), as God taught me, live more closely to the Muslim way of eating than any of the rest of the white civilization.

The Jews and Muslims have always been able to settle their differences between each other better than Christians and Muslims. The Meccan white Muslims claim to be first cousins to the Black Man through Abraham's two sons (Ishmael and Isaac). But, never-theless, among the three parties now (Muslims, Jews, and Christians)—and a fourth party (Hindus) a great conflict arises and is growing to reach a bitter end if wisdom is not found to curb it. But, the American Jew and the American Black Man may yet find some way of making a separate relationship out of the other world.

Eat the natural food and do not try eating all of it at one time. Do not seek to "gobble" down all the refined sugars and sweets that are made from natural foods, lest you find yourself being put in a refined "box" that carries the dead.

Do not feed your children all sorts of processed foods (such as cereals), IF you can give them fresh foods. And do not give your child ready-prepared food. Prepare it yourself as mother used to do a long time ago. You were more healthy in those days than you are now. Prepare your child's food and give it to him; but do not feed it to him out of your mouth as grandmother used to do (smile). But still, we survived from that bet-ter than we are surviving from these processed foods today.

A SICK mother's milk is better for her baby than a healthy cow's milk or any animal's milk. You may give your babies cow milk, but if you can breast-feed them, yourself—as nature intended—then you should do so. You will have a healthier baby and a baby who will love you. When a baby is nursed on cows' milk, the baby may love the cow more than he loves you. (smile)

EAT GOOD FOOD so that you will be able to give your baby good, pure milk.

You can drink cows' milk; your own milk glands will put it into the right stage for your child. Be careful as to what kind of drugs you take while nursing your baby. And do not take fasts while you are breast-feeding an infant or even while you are pregnant. If you like, you may eat once a day while pregnant or breast-feeding your baby, but you are not forced to do so. You should not go for two or three days without eating.

IN ANSWER to your questions on wholewheat cakes and muffins: Yes, you may eat them. But do not eat them or any bread the same day you bake it if you can avoid doing so. Do not eat fresh, hot muffin rings and hot cakes because they are half-cooked breads. Everything in the line of breads should be thoroughly cooked. There is no such thing as stale bread. The bread you call stale bread is the bread you should eat.

When children suffer from bronchial-asthma or any asthmatic conditions, do not give them too much milk. Give them more fruit and juices; (fresh juices, not canned juices).

Adults should try to eat one meal a day. If you eat one meal every two days, three days or five days it is okay, but do not force children under 16 years of age to do the same. They are growing and most of them need two meals a day.

The scientists of this world (the white race) failing to gain the confidence of the people ran a race of commercialization between each other. This commercializing on foods has put forbidden, divinely forbidden, and poison foods on the market for human consumption. Now these poison foods have created another commercial field (drugs) to temporarily reduce the effect of the poison foods eaten by the people, that they purchase from the food markets. Therefore the health and span of good happy lives without drugs of the whole white race and the Black people who are under the rule of the white race are being destroyed by the artificial and poison foods put on sale in the market (which is backed by the government and communities to be eaten by human beings for the sake of that "commercialized dollar").

SUGAR—For an instance, sweets and meats have become the greatest desire "dishes" of America. Food is eaten with many artificial flavors and colorings (slow death) added. There is no need to draw sweets out of sugar cane and sugar beets to sweeten other foods that we eat when by nature all foods that we eat have some natural sugar or sweetening in them. Even meats are sweet enough for our taste and digestion. A little salt added and a little pure pepper added to make it taste hot is sufficient. The other flavors are not necessary.

FRUITS—Fruits are all good and best for our consumption in their natural state. Fruits should never be cooked to get the better value out of them for our health. Fruits should be eaten raw and not cooked. The drying of fruits is only for preservation so that it can be

eaten later but not with the value that it contained
when it was fresh.

CHAPTER TWENTY FIVE
FOOD ROBBED OF NATURAL VITAMINS

We must be careful of what we put in our stomachs because what we put in our stomachs will maintain life and it will take life away.

THE WORLD THAT WE ARE now living in, as I have repeatedly written in this article, is a commercial world, which commercializes on everything on which they can make an extra dollar.

The food that we eat is robbed of its natural vitamins and proteins. Do you want some vitamins and proteins? Go to the drugstores. There, you will find them on the shelves in the drugstores in pills and in liquid form.

Now, you may eat a lot of what you used to think was good "vitamin and protein" food but those vitamins and proteins are not there in the food anymore.

When the vitamins and proteins have been taken from natural food (where nature put them and where they should be eaten) you then do not have the original pure vitamins and proteins.

When the vitamins and proteins are chemically taken out of natural foods, it makes the food less valuable. The chemicals used to take out vitamins and proteins from their natural place in food and the chemicals used to keep and preserve the vitamins and proteins make it not too safe for us to eat vitamins and proteins in pills and liquid form.

It is a pity that the good food is robbed for the sake of a commercial dollar.

CHAPTER TWENTY SIX

DO NOT IGNORE DIVINE LAW

IT IS very hard to find pure food that is not poisoned by the enemy for the purpose of making it unfit for our lives, when the enemy has access to the food and freedom to do so. He admits that he has poisoned the poor old cow's grass and now has poisoned the water and the atmosphere, which is also hunting him. It is a shame. But, as David says in his Psalms, let them be caught in the trap that they set for others.

A MAN should pay for such evil planning against innocent people. He should suffer the same as that which he would like for the people to suffer.

WE HAVE a Just God on the scene today, and His Greatest Desire is to Make everyone bear the consequences of their own evils. For the American white people to do such evil things against the lives of men and of animals, beasts and fowls, is a dirty shame.

EATING one meal a day will prolong your life. Try and get the best foods you can. And, eat it in the Name of Allah. This will prolong your life. If you eat one meal every two days (every 48 hours), you are adding more days to your life than when you eat 24 hours. But, get away from that hog. Get away from grinding out your stomach with rough corn bread and with peanuts and all kinds of nuts. Keep these things out of your stomach. They will kill you and shorten your life, and will cause you to start looking old quickly.

THIS IS a "nut" civilization (the white world), because of their habits which were taken up four thousand years ago and beyond. When they were in the hillsides and caves of Europe, they ate the foods other wild beasts ate. That is why you see white people eating all kinds of foods today. It is due to their inheriting it from their fathers. As you know, they will eat anything. Only a few of them reach 100 years of age, when they should be reaching two or three hundred years of age. To ignore the Divine Law, which God Has Taught you and me, is to ignore your own life.

EAT TO LIVE. Eat the right foods.

Allah has said that no wild game should be eaten at all. Regardless as to how you love deer meat, the deer is not good to eat. No game that runs wild in the woods or birds that fly, with the exception of baby pigeons that have never flown away from the nest where they were born, (called squabs) should be eaten. Please do not eat coons, opossums, turtles, turtle eggs, or frog legs. None of these are good for us.

MILK AND BREAD that has not been robbed of its value is good for us. If you must have some type of fat take the fat from milk (butter). Cheese is also good for us. Some people will make a meal of cheese and eat it as though they were eating bread. But, we should not eat too much cheese. Please do not eat corn bread, and do not fry your foods.

NO NUTS, whatsoever should be eaten. Allah taught me that they take away five years of your life everytime you eat them. And stop eating that concrete-like peanut butter.

Do not eat popcorn; eat fresh corn in its milk stage (known as milk corn). And do not eat hominy grits.

DO NOT EAT crackers. As long as you have good bread at home, eat your own cooked breads. Eat crackers whenever you are traveling. This kind of food is made to keep you together until you can get to your own cooked foods. Eggs are all right to eat in some cases, but do not try to eat all that the hens lay at one time. (smile).

PIG, PORK OR SWINE

CHAPTER TWENTY-SEVEN

HOG MADE OF CAT, RAT AND DOG

Eat one meal a day or one meal every other day, if you are able to. And, eat the food that Allah has prescribed for us. Stay away from the poison food that dresses the Christian's table. You do not have to eat every variety of food on the earth to be healthy, for two varieties of good food is sufficient.

THERE ARE GOOD vegetables for you to eat and there is good fruit for you to eat. And, if you want some meat, there is some good meat growing out there you can eat without eating the poison meat (the pig). The white man's greatest desire is that you do that which breaks the Divine Law by eating this poison flesh. Everything God says "Thou shall not do," he says "Thou shall do."

You watch him. He is not a friend of God nor is he a doer or a lover of His Law. They were made by nature to be opposers to God and His Law and the righteous people. And, you see them living other than Divine Law.

They are always in trouble; always sick; fighting and disagreeing with each other.

No people should expect peace and contentment who are opposed to the Law of God or obedience to Him that brings us into such conditions of life. Since God has exposed them and exposed the hog, they now will say to you "cook it thoroughly done and it is all right to eat." It is not all right to eat it if you cook it thoroughly and kill every pork worm there is in it. The actual flesh then is still poison and is divinely prohibited flesh that you should not even touch—not to think of eating it, for it was not made to eat. It was made for medical purposes for the white race and I have taught you time and again, that God taught me they did not make the hog to be taken as a food, but made it for medical purposes.

Since there is a poison in it, the flesh of swine will cure most any kind of disease. Take a slice of this "fatty" and "salty" pork and you have a boil on you some place, full of fever; lay a piece of fat on it and it will soon draw it out.

IT IS A MEDICINE and not food. This is not all it will do in a curing way. I do not have time and space here to put this in this article, but the white man knows and he will bear me witness that I am teaching you the truth of this hog. Medical scientists and our own doctors are fast learning, since I have been writing this article on HOW TO EAT TO LIVE and are now co-operating with me and agreeing with me that the hog is a poison that we should not eat, though they may be eating it themselves. But, they have to acknowledge the truth. Some of them are intelligent enough now, for the last few years, to start getting away from eating it.

Who wants to eat the combination of these fleshes: cat, rat, and dog? This is what the hog is made of —the dog, cat and rat, and the Bible teaches you that he is from a mouse. Read Isaiah 66:17 , "They that sanctify themselves, and purify themselves in the gardens behind one tree in the midst, eating swine's flesh, and the abomination, and the mouse, shall be consumed together, saith the Lord."

The so-called American Negro is a product of evil and filth, produced by the white man of slavery. He is more a true believer in the evils and filth of the white man than the white man himself. As it is written (Bible), when he (devil) makes a convert, he makes him seven times more the child of hell than himself. This is the so-called American Negro. He is turned into a person seven times worse than he originally was.

So, do not think that you are Divinely safe eating pork after you think you have cooked it so done you have killed the pork worms in it. The flesh alone—not to say eating it—is Divinely prohibited to touch. This, the white man knows, but what does he care? He eats anything.

EAT TO LIVE AND COME FOLLOW ME.

CHAPTER TWENTY EIGHT

HOG DIVINELY PROHIBITED

Eat one meal a day of good food that Allah (God) prescribes for us.

Strict Orthodox Jews follow the law that Allah gave to Moses on what food to eat and those strict Jews will not eat the prohibited foods that Allah made prohibited. So, their food is good for you, Allah teaches us in the Holy Qur-an. And, the strict Muslim food is good for the Jew.

TOUCH NOT that which Allah has forbidden to be touched. There are many tricks that the devil is play - ing on the total population in our foods and drinks so we have to be on our guard when we go to the market to purchase our food.

There are some people who love to eat poison foods and drinks and they write me trying to defend themselves in eating other than good foods. One writer asked me a question on the eating of hog for cure. Sometime ago, I wrote that the white race is saying if you cook it (the hog) thoroughly done, you are destroying this pork worm in it. But, I also remind you that the very flesh is Divinely prohibited and that you should not even touch the flesh—not to think of eating it.

Regardless to how long you cook it, you still should not eat it.

CHAPTER TWENTY NINE
SWINE EATS ANYTHING

The safest way of all to eat, is to stop eating so often (three meals a day and meals between those three meals). In the past, our appetites were as the appetites of swine. The swine has no certain time to eat. It will eat until it is sick and has to lay down, but as soon as it finds a vacancy in its stomach, it eats more food. It doesn't matter what kind of food it may be; the swine eats anything. The swine's life is very short, because it comes here eating itself to death and death soon takes it away.

WE EAT TOO much too often, and we eat the wrong foods (poison foods). Most of our drinks are poison.

Allah has blessed America with the best of foods and with good water that is plentiful. America has been blessed with everything that she could desire, but after all of these blessings, she is ungrateful and turns good things into bad, and wages a war against the God of good and His People.

After telling the slaves they were free, America kept them here in order to prey upon them. Now today, many of the slaves wish to be free of America, but her reply by her actions to our wanting to be free is "no." And America continues to give the so-called Negroes the same bad food and drink that her (America's) fathers did in the days of servitude slavery.

AMERICA'S markets are loaded with swine, and loaded with vegetables and fruits which are preserved and made to look beautiful by having poison chemicals poured upon them. There are thousands, tens of thousands, and hundreds of thousands of herds of cattle and there are hundreds of thousands of fowls. Yet, Americans decorate their tables with the divinely prohibited flesh—the swine, and represent themselves as being the true Christian followers of Jesus.

Americans have poison whiskey and wine by the barrels and vats all over the country, yet when this does not make them intoxicated (drunk) and crazy enough, they resort to drugs (the poison weeds).

ALLAH HAS blessed them with so much bread that they set whole fields of good wheat on fire. They burn up the wheat in order to obtain higher prices for it. They are crazy over money and wealth.

Now today, Allah threatens America with all kinds of plagues—not one kind, but many kinds. Allah withholds the rains from her wheat fields; sends terrific cold and snow upon her fertile bread basket areas; kills her cattle, livestock and fowls; and kills her fish that are inland in ponds and rivers, with droughts.

ALL OF these plagues are falling upon America because she is against God's giving freedom, justice and equality to the so-called Negroes, whose labor she has had for 400 years. Because of America's having broken the Divine Law which prohibits eating swine flesh, and because of her having fed this forbidden meat to her slaves and to other nations of the earth, Allah (God), is now taking His blessings away from her.

CHAPTER THIRTY
PORK CONTAINS WORMS
(TRICHINAE)

Eat one meal a day or one meal every two days, if you are able. If you eat the proper food, and not poison food and drink, you will prolong your life, make your-self youthful, and will keep away sickness, and suffering (even colds), said Allah to me in the Person of Master Fard Muhammad, to Whom praises are due forever.

KEEP THE body and the mind clean. Do good to self and to others. Keep away from evil and remember Allah always, and He Who Came in the Person of Master Fard Muhammad, to Whom praises are due forever, will remember you. But, you must eat pure food (the food that Allah has pointed out to us to eat) and stay away from that which He Forbids us to eat, such as swine flesh (the hog).

I will be a happy man when I see the day that our Black people forsake the hog. This divinely prohibited flesh (the swine) can be the cause of most of our sick-ness. The professional people, such as doctors and religious scholars and scientists, know this to be true. But, in this wicked world (of the white race) they were made to teach against the good Law and Guidance of Almighty God, Allah, to Whom praises are due for-ever.

ALL THAT God Says "thou shall not do" the white race says "thou shall do," or "thou should do." And then, they are bold enough to ask you "what is wrong with eating pig."

The hog, according to the teachings of God, in the Person of Master Fard Muhammad, to Whom praises are due forever, is very poisonous. It contains more poison than a rattlesnake. Of course white people eat rattlesnakes. It is not the flesh of the rattlesnake which is so poisonous, but the sac full of poison, which it carries in its mouth. When the rattlesnake strikes it empties the sac of poison into your flesh. This causes death to the victim, if he does not receive attention quickly. But, the actual flesh of the hog is 999% poison (nearly 1000%) as taught to me by God, in the Person of Master Fard Muhammad, to Whom praises are due forever. This poison is not going to kill you instantly. It drags you along for many years.

IT IS a very deceitful poison. It is in the form of live worms commonly called pork worms (trichinae). In a hog eater's body, these worms multiply by the millions. They first enter the walls of the stomach and then from the stomach pass out into the intestinal walls. And, from the intestines they travel up the back in the spinal cord into the muscles of the body and finally into the brain. When these worms get into these two places, last mentioned (of the body), the disease becomes incurable.

Look at the pictures in physiology books or in the dictionary where this worm is enlarged several hundred times. The lives of people with such poisonous worms in their bodies are usually limited to less than one hundred years, and for many, less than seventy years. There are a few who live past a hundred years, whose constitutions may have been much stronger than others.

YOU MAY say, "one hundred years is all I would want to live." No, this is not the Truth. You would like to live a hundred thousand years if you could, when death approaches you, for this is the law of life; it always wants to stay here.

Eating any kind of flesh is not good for us, not even beef. No animal flesh can be said to be good for human consumption, not even fowls, and very few fish, not to think of the scavengers of the waters, such as crabs, shrimps and oysters.

We must learn to eat vegetables and fruits and stay away from land flesh. It is a little difficult for us to suddenly stop eating beef, lamb, and chicken, but we must wean away from such flesh gradually.

EATING one meal a day prolongs your life if you eat the right food. People will soon live a life of one thousand years, after the removal of this wicked world.

CHAPTER THIRTY ONE

THE TRUTH ABOUT PORK (THE PIG)

Pork or pig, all its parts and by-products, has been a chief food for the so-called American Negro since the days of his physical bondage. The pig was not made for human consumption. The pig is the chief cause of many of the ills and mental deficiencies occuring among the so-called American Negroes and any other people who eat it.

The pig is a mass of worms. Each mouthful you eat is not a nutritious food but a mass of small worms the naked eye cannot detect. Worms thrive in the hog. When these worms are digested into your system, they cause a high birth rate to hundreds of new worms called larvae which travels the blood stream of your system and lodge in your muscles. These worms even enter your brain, lungs or your spinal fluid. They cause muscular aches, fever and many other symptoms of sickness. The worm has an amazing ability to go undetected in your system for many years.

The scientific name for the ill-causing worm found in all pork is Trichinella spiralis which causes trichinosis.

Despite what veterinarians, public health officals, the Agricultural Department or your doctor say, the best defense against the pig is DO NOT EAT IT! When you do eat it, you do not hurt God, His Messenger, the Muslim or anyone else. You hurt yourself.

Thorough and slow cooking of pork does not remove the danger of the worms found in all pork. Additional cooking of pork purchased in the summer or processed pork products does not make the worm-infested pork safe for eating.

Inspection and governmental seals on pork do not remove the danger of the worms yet in the pork to make it safe for you to eat.

Some say never taste raw sausage or any raw pork. It is best not to eat pork, raw, processed, cooked, smoked, cured, or seasoned.

You are what you eat, so why not eat the best and be the best. Do not allow this rotten, diseased meat to be sold in your neighborhoods or brought into your homes.

Pork is often referred to as "cured." The word "cured" is the past tense of the verb "cure." If a meat has to be cured before we eat it, we should not even take the chance to eat it.

In the Bible and the Holy Quran, it is the Divine will of God that the pig should not be eaten and God has never changed this instruction, despite the white man's setting up governmental bureaus to grade and approve the selling of pork.

The so-called Negroes should ban this meat from their communities and all those who sell and eat it!

CHAPTER THIRTY TWO

KNOW TRUTH ABOUT FLESH OF THE SWINE

I told you how Allah taught me the birth of the swine, and for the purpose for making this animal only was for the whites. Because of their being a grafted race, they were made weaker, physically, through the man from whom they came (the Black man). Since the body of the grafted is weaker than the original body, it would be easier for them to attract germs than the original man. You should not argue with me about this because all of the diseases that trouble us today — from social disease to cancer — came from the white race, one way or another.

Do not tell me about four or five hundred years or one thousand years; I am referring to this people's entire historical scope. They have had 6,000 years to mix and poison our people. Some of you are foolish enough to accept all the blame. But God clears you of it. This refers to those who love the devils so well they would like to dispute God about them. I am teaching, only, you the truth—take it or leave it.

They are too wise to dispute the truth. Read the story in the Bible where Jesus met a man who was possessed of evil spirits. When the evil spirits recognized Jesus to be from God—knowing they would have no chance to contend with him over their presence in the man where they did not belong—they pleaded with Jesus to let them go into the swine, and Jesus agreed. The man who was possessed of evil spirits was none other than the American so-called Negroes. The evil spirits in them are from the white race, making them eat the divinely-prohibited flesh of the swine. The devils were allowed to go into the swine. They ran down a steep place into a lake or sea and perished.

Here the picture changes; the meaning changes a bit. The hog was made for the white race for medical purposes—not even for them to eat it—but they could eat it if they wanted to, since they were created to be destroyed. They use this hog in much of their medical preparation, even to the German 606 (606 poison germs).

Allah taught me that one of these germs came from the swine. However, the white man will advise you to eat it. He would have you think the swine is cleaner now than he was in Jesus' time, but wouldn't God know—4,000 years from Moses—if this swine would be clear of poison? You admit God is a Fore-knower.

The whole story was twisted around. They want you to think God did not know about this process of the devils leaving the man and entering the swine until after it happened. Actually, God knew it was going to happen before it took place. Using deceit, they have succeeded in getting you to eat the swine as food, though it was made to produce a poisonous germ for medical purposes in curing the diseases of the white race.

This is how he makes you to break all of the com-mandments of God. Because he is God's enemy and yours and mine, he has you breaking the divine law. We did this because we saw him doing it and at that time had no teacher of our own. These are the tricks of your hidden enemies and their own concocted religion called Christianity, which is deceiving and leading you to your doom with them.

I am your brother, and Allah has revealed to me the truth for your salvation. Jesus also prophesied that the truth would free you—that is, if you accept the truth. The thing you must understand in this parable of Jesus is that, actually, the visible swine could not have gone crazy and choked in the sea or lake, because of the spirit of the devil was sent in them in the meaning that Jesus wants you to understand. The swine that was choked to death in the sea after the spirit of the devil was taken out of the man, the believers among the so-called American Negroes, and the swine that ran into the lake and perished, is the disbelievers among the so-called Negroes who refuse to accept the truth. They will be cast alive in a lake of fire with the devils.

As you have in the Bible, Lucifer's (Yakub) fall also represents the fall of his race. The lake or sea in which they choked and perished, is the same lake mentioned in the Revelations of John—that all that had the mark of the beast, the representatives of the beast and the false prophets (priests and preachers of Christianity) referred to as being cast alive in a lake of fire.

I hope you understand. What I am trying to get over is that you who reject Allah and His true religion—entire submission to His will as the Arabs call it, Islam—will perish in the lake of fire with this race of adversaries of Allah and His true religion, to which they refuse to submit. They now are trying to woo you into sharing hell-fire with them, though they know that you have a chance to go to heaven while they do not.

I cannot force you to halt your down-hill plunge with them into the lake of fire. I only have been missioned to warn you in the simplest language. I cannot force you to go to hell or heaven.

Your sweethearting and wanting to marry them is like a frog trying to court a rattlesnake. The rattle-snake gives the frog freedom to do so because he intends to swallow the frog. Taking the death dealing pill and the knife to destroy your future generations are examples. Socializing with them is no sign of justice, but a sign that they have deceived you into going to hell with them. Take it leave it.

CHAPTER THIRTY THREE

STOP EATING IT (PIG)

I think we have said enough about the poison animal called, in Arabic, khanzier (khan meaning, "I see," and zier meaning "very foul"). Beyond a shadow of a doubt the swine is the filthiest and foulest animal human beings could have resorted to for food. The flesh of the swine, while cooking, has a very different smell from that of other animal's flesh while cooking. And even when it is not being cooked, it is full of worms.

In many cases, the eater of the flesh becomes nauseated when the flesh is being fried in the early morning. It is a divinely prohibited flesh and God (Allah) has prohibited you and me, my Brothers and Sisters of the Black Nation, from eating it or even touching its dead carcass.

Please, for our health's sake, stop eating it; for our beauty's sake, stop eating it; for our obedience to God and His Laws against this flesh, stop eating it; for a longer life, stop eating it and for the sake of modesty, stop eating it.

Do you know, that if we, the 22 million lost-found members of our Nation here, in America, would stop eating this pig, (his poison swine flesh), it would mean a great economic savings to us? And I do not think the government would be so eager to eat it themselves if we would obey this Divine law against the divinely prohibited flesh. There is an old, foolish answer our people have given to such advice: "The white folks eat it, and my grandparents ate it, and they lived to be 75 and 80 years old.''

If Noah and Methuselah had heard you boasting that your parents lived only 75 or 80 years eating poison, they would have considered your parents as never having grown up to become adults, according to their good way of eating the best food, about twice a week, and living nearly 1,000 of our present calendar years which consists of 365 days.

God does not punish us for the crime of disobedience to His law if we are ignorant of His laws. But after knowledge of His laws, He is justified in punishing us by setting the full penalty according to the disobedience.

As I have previously said in this book, most vegetables that are sold on the public market are good to eat with the exception of those Allah prohibits, such as collard greens and the rough turnip salads. You have plenty of other vegetables to eat. And, you have good peas other than lima beans; field butter beans, called baby lima beans, and black eyed peas (field peas as we called them).

Eat the good fruit and the good vegetables according to your condition. Some of us cannot eat even the best of these because of the condition of our health.

You are your judge there.

CHAPTER THIRTY FOUR

HOG

One woman judge in Washington, standing against the force-feeding of the swine to the Muslims through their food was one of the voices against pork that I have ever read. The eating of swine flesh is against the Christian religion according to its teachings. The Christians make this swine flesh a prohibited flesh among their own religion, but then they force it on another religious group. This shows the hypocrisy of the Christians.

It is in papers that they transport all over the world for people to read and follow after, while they, themselves, are not following it. It is in the Bible where we have so much against the eating of the swine flesh, and it goes so far as to teach against even touching the carcass of the swine. But, in Christian America, selling and eating swine is one of the greatest markets that she has. The hog is sacrificed in the church, is barbecued on the church grounds, and they ask the God's Blessings on the curse that He Made against eating the hog. This action of the Christians is one of the most open condemnations of the law and rules that they represent against using this Divinely prohibited flesh of the hog.

They glorify the eating of the hog as though God is with them to eat what He has made a curse, as Isaiah mentioned it, they called themselves in eating hog (Bible 66:17). Now here comes the Muslims who have been the slaves of Christian America, wanting to obey the Bible, but they are tried by force to not obey the Bible. The Brotherhood of the Muslims is what Paul and his Epistles preached; the Brotherhood gets to clear sunshine.

Christian America is not Christian, because Christian means to be one and one in Christ. Everything that the Bible teaches is against the Divine Law of God, is practiced by the Christians.

I think this judge, Mrs. Burnita Shelton Matthews should be given credit not only by us, the Muslims, but by the world of Christianity; as she is not speaking so much in our favour as she is speaking to Christians who are failing to do these things themselves. Stay away from the swine, instead of trying to force the swine on others. The Christian religion teaches the same against the eating and partaking of the swine flesh.

CHAPTER THIRTY FIVE

THE PIG IS POISON

Do not eat the swine. Do not use any form of tobacco. Do not smoke it or chew it. According to medical scientists, the tobacco weed affects the whole body. The heart, lungs, liver, kidney and bladder can be affected by the use of tobacco.

WOULD THE government like for you to stop using the tobacco weed—yes or no? The government harvests a great revenue from the tax on tobacco, therefore, it would not like to stop its citizens from using tobacco. But, if the taxpayer is losing his life by producing and using the tobacco weed, the government, yet, will not win.

The poor man who uses quite a bit of tobacco and is not able to pay the doctor's bill for the harm that the tobacco will'cause in his body, may have to go on charity. The taxpayers will have to pay the doctor's bill to cure the illnesses that are caused by using tobacco.

So, it does not make sense for the government to continue to allow the citizens of its country to use a poison that it knows is gradually taking the lives of its citizens.

THE PIG IS another poison people are eating. The government takes no steps towards stopping the raising of swine to be marketed for the people to eat, because it is another thing that brings much money to the government. But all the medical scientists know the hog should not be eaten as food by anyone.

It just shows how wicked the Christian race is. They preach "Thou shall not do this" and point it out in their religious book (Bible) and yet they are the ones who are breaking every forbidden thing of their law.

But, since we now have been given the truth from the mouth of God of this race of people—that they are not what we thought they were and that they are only a race of devils by nature—why should we expect anything from the devils but evil? They cannot be devils and be good.

WE HAVE been made so blind, deaf, and dumb to knowing the people who have exercised rule and authority over us. We have wondered, time and again, why they treat us so wickedly.

But now we have been taught from the mouth of God the true knowledge of this people and ourselves, why should we be so foolish now to continue to follow them for right guidance? They could not guide us rightly, when by nature they were created to deceive and mislead.

The Bible is full of the teachings of the true knowledge of the nature of the devil, from Genesis to the Revelations, but we did not understand the Bible. Now, the truth has come and the knowledge of the book (Bible) has been made known.

SO, EAT THE good food that Allah (God) has given to us and stay away from the things that are no good and poison.

MEAT, BEASTS, OR FLESH

CHAPTER THIRTY SIX

NO MEAT IS GOOD FOR US

It is true and understandable that we live in a poison world—poison food, poison drinks, and poison spiritual food. The three mentioned above are the base of our life. Our lives depend upon them.

WE MUST again remember that the enemies of God and Righteousness, do not follow the path of righteousness in any way. They were made to form the teachings of their own. They could not have been the God of this world. If they had followed the World teachings and guidance, they would not have been an enemy of ours. But, since they had to build a world different from ours, they did so. Do not think hard of them for doing that which they were made by nature to do. We have to be careful.

Here is a good example that they did not intend to follow the course of our God, The God of Truth, Freedom, Justice, and Equality. In the Bible, Moses forbade them from eating the swine: "Thou shall not eat the swine, nor touch its carcass." He says just the reverse; he challenges God by saying, "What is wrong with the hog?" "Thou shall eat it." And, he fills his markets throughout the world with that divinely prohibited flesh, the hog. And, 90 per cent of the people follow them in breaking that law and everything else.

If you will study it, you will see that if God says Thou shall not do, he says thou shall do. God says do not swear or curse, the Bible then teaches that their mouths are full of swearing and cursing. He is truthfully a made devil, and we must take him for that. But, he would like to deceive us (the Righteous) in order to get us to follow him.

I say, eat the best of the food. The Orthodox Jews are right when they do not eat the hog and other poison foods, and if you buy from their markets, you will get the better foods. I do not make any mistake; I mean the Orthodox Jews, who do not carry in their markets the type of poison foods consumed by the Christians.

BUT, ONE thing that we should remember is that we can produce our own foods if we can get into the earth to produce our own. Good whole beans and good whole milk and butter is fine for us. And, if we eat meat, do not make a habit of eating a lot of beef. Eat lamb and sheep. As I have said time and again, that no meat is good for us, but we eat it, so that which we eat, try to eat the best of it.

CHAPTER THIRTY SEVEN
EAT TO LIVE AND NOT TO DIE

Of all the thousands and tens of thousands of instruction items on health issued by doctors and scientists regarding the type of food that we should eat, none of them is equal to the way that Allah—in the Person of Master Fard Muhammad, to Whom Praise is due forever—has taught us.

Eating one meal a day, one meal every other day or one meal every three days is a better way to obtain good health and long life than all of the tens of thousands of pamphlets and books authored by doctors, quack doctors and would-be doctors. The divine points out the best way that will produce good health.

We should not stuff our stomachs with food just because we have the food to put in our stomachs three times a day.

Some people are foolish enough to think eating three or four times a day is really the way to obtain good health—but take a second thought of what you are doing. You keep your stomach working all the time trying to digest the surplus food for which your stomach has not even asked.

He, Master Fard Muhammad (God in Person), taught me never to eat when I am not hungry. He taught me to wait until I am fully hungry—then to eat until I am full and not to eat again until I am really hungry. This is common sense.

The pig eats all the time; the chicken eats all the time- as long as you give them food to eat—and their span of life is significantly short.

The dog is greedy, but the hog is greedier. The dog will stop eating when it has eaten enough. If you continue to feed it, it will try to store the food until such time that it is hungry.

Often, you hear people say, "Come on and eat" and one will say, "I am not hungry." The reply is : "Eat before you get hungry." This is most unwise. It is inviting sickness and death.

The mucous-forming foods eaten by the people should be replaced with such less mucous-forming foods as plenty of vegetables and fruits.

Whole wheat bread should be eaten instead of white bread, which is mucous-forming.

Let us try not to eat so much meat — especially animal flesh. No meat is good for good health and longevity. We must stop eating meat gradually, because actually, meat is not by nature a food for human consumption.

Eating one meal once a day or once every two days, with no meals between, gives the body time to rest the digestive machinery after the previous meal— and this gives the blood time to purify itself of the poison from the last meal.

After three days without taking food into the body, the blood is found to be in much better condition.

Let us see if we can gradually stop eating animal flesh and chickens or fowls of any kind.

Eat to live and not to die.

CHAPTER THIRTY EIGHT

They Eat As The Beast Eats (Holy Qur-an)

Since the time of Moses (4000 years ago), we have followed the way of life taught to us by the white race, which often is referred to now in the religious language as the Christian race.

The practice of eating by the white race is not accepted anymore by the people of Islam, to bring to the people a better health and longer life. It must begin with what they eat and how often they force the body to partake of foods for which their appetites call.

A slight reflection on the eating habits of the Christians and what they eat is enough for you and me to know that one's life would be limited to less than 100 years by such eating habits.

The sign in the Bible by David (Psalms) limits the life of the wicked to three score and 10 years (seventy years) and in another place (In the Psalms) he says that the wicked live not half of their days.

We have history on what they made of themselves. Their history was written before they came into existence (or were made), which speaks the truth of what they would be (Holy Qur-an).

They have not, as yet, done anything as a surprise to Allah and the scientists.

In fact, as Allah taught me that the scientists of Islam write all of our life histories on what we will do, even to the name of any outstanding person among us, 25,000 years in the future. In this way, they must respect the knowledge of fore-knowledge of God.

We cannot blame the white race for its way of civilization, which already was written and we cannot blame them for their way of civilization because it is not like ours, because they are not of us. They are a new people made among us with the nature, training and teaching of their father to do just what they are doing. They cannot help themselves, many of them would like to do differently, but they cannot do that which they are by nature not made to do.

Their way of eating like the beast is true. They eat just about all of the time—three, four or more times a day and even between meals. This is the nature of a beast and especially the hog and dog. They will accept food whether or not they can swallow it and they will eat until they cannot swallow. There are other animals (Beasts) of similar characteristics, but the swine and the dog are the greediest of all.

The white race is mentioned in a teaching of the Bible in St. Mark, Chapter 5:13, in the evil spirits taken out of the man, mentioned there of being possessed with evil spirits and the spirits begging Jesus to allow them to go into the hog. Here, the two are associated with each other—the evil spirits and the hog.

The hog was not made evil by nature, but by nature, it was made to serve the evil person. Therefore, both were made for each other.

CHAPTER THIRTY NINE

ANIMAL FLESH?

HOW TO EAT TO LIVE is one of the best and greatest of advice to give to a person or a people. Why did we get out of the knowledge of HOW TO EAT TO LIVE? Our loss of knowledge of HOW TO EAT TO LIVE was due to the fact that we were living under the temporary rule of gods (white race) whose nature was not like ours. Since it is the nature of the white race to do the opposite of right and to oppose the natural Good Law of the God of the Righteous, this caused the wrong foods to be eaten by the eater. Therefore we have been eating the wrong food under the rule of the white race.

REMEMBER the Bible's symbol like language (in Genesis) of the made-man (serpent, devil) talking to Eve, who represents the righteous. The made-man (serpent) condemned what God had said to Eve and he (wrongly) accused the God of trying to deprive Eve of knowledge that she should have. However, Eve should have known the difference between the evil and the good and she should not have taken the serpent (devil) for a guide.

TAKING the man-made (devil) for a guide is the mistake that the Lost-Found Black People has made and continues to make. They take the opposer of God to be their right-guide.

ALLAH (God) Who Came in the Person of Master Fard Muhammad, to Whom Praises are due forever, said to me, "Eat one meal a day and eat the right kind of food in that meal." Animal flesh? NO. But we are not committing a sin by eating animal flesh if we cannot help ourselves. But DO NOT EAT THE HOG, by any means. Even if we are starving we should not eat the flesh of the hog.

Originally, the hog was not on our planet. The hog was made after the making of the made-man (white man) and he was made for the made-man; the hog was not made for the Original Man (Black Man).

THE famous meats that the Black Man eats are beef and lamb. We eat chicken and fowl, but they are not good for us nor are birds good for us to eat, except that young pigeon which we call the squab. The squab is good to eat when it is young and has not yet flown from its nest, but when the squab flies from his nest, do not eat him.

BEFORE the making of the white man the Black Man did not eat animal flesh. After the removal of the white man, there will be no more eating of this type of meat (animal flesh or even fowl). There will be a complete stoppage and practice of the eating of land flesh regardless to whether it is animal, beast or fowl. The people will live a thousand years without eating them.

CHAPTER FORTY
MEAT NEVER INTENDED
FOR MAN TO EAT

Eat one meal per day—nothing between meals and eat the right food.

We eat meat but meat was never intended for man to eat from the very creation of man. We have been eating meat. Why? Because the ruler of this nation of earth for the past six thousand years (6,000 years) is an enemy of the Original Man who has inhabited the earth from time unknown to man. A people that have been populating the earth here for billions and trillions of years would not eat the wrong food if they had not been made to suffer for guidance under a made enemy of theirs. And, the enemy does not follow what we, the Original Man had and was practicing.

It is true, according to the Teachings of Almighty God to me that he caused us to eat the wrong foods. He is doing it himself and any man (the Original Black Man) who comes into his civilization, he tries to force him to eat the wrong foods. I have seen him doing this and, we whom he reared himself and had the power over us after destroying the knowledge of self from us.

The white race or the Caucasian or devil eats all kinds of poison: frogs, snakes, and all filthy scavengers of water. He eats it and invites you to eat it but they know it is not good. He eats all kinds of fowls, he knows they are not good for us to eat—and wild fowls at that. And, he eats wild animals and beasts of the jungles. That which he digs up out of the earth of the live creatures that live under the earth's surface, he knows that it is not good to eat (for himself and you too) but he advertises it that it is all right to eat. Everything he eats, he tells you it is all right. So, if you follow the white race's food eating, you are bound to eat the wrong food for your consumption. So, I warn you against the food of this race.

They do not eat the good food because they found us eating the good food and to make a world different from ours, they had to resort to eating the wrong food so that they could say that they established something which we did not have or were not doing.

The Holy Qur-an Refers to the white man as eating like a beast. They eat as the beasts. This is true; they do not deny it.

The Bible teaches us against eating their dainty meats, which is a warning that you may be eating the wrong meat.

Since they learned that their time was limited among us on earth, they have studied everything possible that was an enemy to us to make us to accept that enemy and like the enemy.

The old filthy hog was not made to be taken as food for us, nor them. Allah Taught me from His Mouth that they made hog for medical purposes. Since he was a weak human being, created for the purpose of weakening the strong Black Man in every way possible, they knew he was going to carry lots of diseases because of the essence that they were made out of themselves (the weak germ of the Original Black Man).

These thousands of different kinds of foods that

he offers you, be aware that they are not to keep you alive, but to kill you. Do not think that they are following the right way by eating that which he himself eats.

Do not eat that which this book has warned you not to eat. And, do not eat like the beasts (every hour or two or whenever food is offered to them, they will eat it). How can you live, eating poison and keeping your stomach trying to digest food 24 hours per day? More next time. HOW TO EAT TO LIVE: One Meal Per Day.

PROPER FOOD
PREPARATION

CHAPTER FORTY ONE

COOK THOROUGHLY DONE

Milk and bread are our best foods. Milk is our first food; bread is next.

Man has been drinking milk continuously through-out his life—from cows, sheep, goats, camels, and buffalo. Since we still crave for this food, and drink it (for after leaving our mother's breast, we go to the breast of cattle the balance of our lives) we should raise these cattle under the most protected eye for their good health.

THE PURE milk fat that we call butter should not be mixed with vegetable fats. It should be eaten with-out mixing it, like grandmother, and grandfather ate it. Substitute foods are destroying a great percentage of good health.

Pure wheat makes the best bread. Having the knowledge that bread is easy to digest, we must re-member that to get the best results out of wheat bread we must cook it thoroughly done. This is to prevent it from doing too much rising, which will cause the stretching of the stomach and other intestines.

BROWN THE bread deep as possible—to a color of deep brown. Do not make your rolls and loaves too thick. Make them thin so that the dough can be cooked and browned through and through. If not able to cook it thoroughly, due to its thickness, cook it a second time, by the same process that you did at first.

Add yeast, (a little more than the first time) milk and water to the bread, stir it and let it sit and sour again. Let it rise good, knead it and then put it back into the oven to cook a second time. This second cooking double prepares it for digestion in our stomaches. Cooking the bread a third or fourth time makes it still better.

WE KILL ourselves in the way we prepare our food. We are too hasty in the preparation of our food. Some of the freshly-baked white bread is fancy to the eyes, but it will not do you a fancy good. It will shorten your life and soon kill you.

Take plenty of time to prepare your food the right way for cooking and then cook it right, not in a haste.

THINK about the order of "hot biscuits." This is a foolish way of looking at and taking bread for the stomach, fresh, as soon as it comes out of the oven. No bread cooked the first day should be eaten that same day. You should wait a couple of days before eating it.

There is no such thing as stale bread. Get away from this belief. The older the bread the better it is for your life. The little molds on the bread are not poison. Brush it off and eat the bread and if you eat some of the mold, it will not harm you.

BACK 50, 60 or more years ago—when people did not take time to prepare their bread right (many did not use yeast, they used a kind of baking powder)— they were made sick time and again from the hasty preparation and eating of this bread.

Many of our people fry dough on top of the stove, "pancake," (slang, flap jacks). This bread, which you put in your stomachs to be digested, is hardly done. If you could look at it working in the stomach, it would look as raw as it did before you put it on the stove. This is hard work on the digestive system.

PLEASE cook your bread thoroughly done. Whatever bread you eat, never eat it freshly cooked, i.e.
the same day that it is cooked.

If you toast today's bread, you should let it brown
to a deep color, almost a burn, so that it will be easily
digested.

CHAPTER FORTY TWO

EAT PROPERLY PREPARED FOOD

The great cause of our illnessess is not eating right and eating too often.

ALLAH (GOD) wants us to live longer and the only way that He can lengthen our lives is by us obeying Him and eating right.

You will feel remarkably better if you would just eat one meal a day. Do not try to start eating one meal every two or three days at first, because you may not keep it up. First try to get used to eating one meal a day.

These are important things to remember—to obtain and maintain good health and long life. Do not eat too much food at any time. Do not eat too frequently. Eat the properly prepared right kind of food.

EATING ONE meal a day or one meal every other day is the key to long life—if you eat the right kind of food. The right kind of food has been described in this article many times.

Cook your food done, but not to a "mush."

Stay away from the hog. And stay away from those "old blackeyed peas," field peas, lima beans, baby butter beans (which are nothing but baby lima beans) and corn bread. Keep them off your table.

CORN BREAD CAN be eaten, but you may not want to prepare it as it should be prepared. Allah (God), in the Person of Master Fard Muhammad, to Whom praise is due forever, taught me that corn bread should be baked two or three times and put away and soured each time with yeast. Let it set in your mold two or three times. You should bake it and sour it again. And Allah (God) said you should put onions in the dough. So, I think you should be very careful in preparing corn bread for eating. It requires a lot of baking.

If you want to add flour to the corn meal, do not use white flour. Use 100 per cent rye flour.

WHEN YOU BAKE rye bread, or prepare corn bread, let it rise two or three times with yeast, bake it, let it set, and then add more yeast to it and bake it a second time. You do not have to add any additional flour or meal to rye flour.

There are many vegetables that you can eat, but please do not eat the wrong vegetables.

CHAPTER FORTY THREE

COOK FOOD CORRECTLY

In this poison world, there are scientists who are experimenting with poison and are experimenting on how to kill or maim people so that they will die later from eating the wrong foods and from breathing this poison atmosphere. It is very hard for a person who wants to eat the proper food to find anything like good food in this poison world, so that his life may be prolonged, because such people as the scientists have poisoned the food.

Eating one meal a day most certainly will prolong our lives if we eat the proper food. Cooking food correctly is another problem that must be solved with you. Regardless to the length of time allowed between each meal and regardless to the knowledge of the best foods to purchase from the markets, if it is not prepared properly, it also will shorten our lives. We must know how to prepare the proper foods so that it may prolong our lives. These people (white race) have been bent on the destruction of our lives and they are the rulers of the land. It is hard to try to eat properly while living right in the midst of such people.

Think over it—that their food scientists teach how to rob food of its value and then put it in pills and in liquid forms to commercialize on. How then, can you eat to live with what he leaves you to eat— foods robbed of their natural vitamins?

DOCTORS, SICKNESS
AND HEALTH

CHAPTER FORTY FOUR
YOU CANNOT REPLACE STOMACH

We must remember that if we are to live, it depends on what we eat and drink. And, God Has Taught us, in the Person of Master Fard Muhammad, To Whom Praises are Due forever, how to eat to live: One meal a day and eat the proper food. Of course, if you are sick, you are not required to do this (eating one meal a day), because the illness takes away energy that we should have to fight the sickness. One meal a day, eating the proper food, will give us the right to live.

We cannot expect to live, if we don't try doing the thing that God Advises us to do to live. We must remember, Allah Comes with light and life to add more days to our life. And, the only way we can enjoy longer life, we have to obey the teaching of how to live.

High blood pressure, diabetes, colds and fevers, ailments of the heart, headaches, stomach aches and all types of ulcers can be cured and vanish under the right food and time that we should eat.

Drink good milk—good, fresh milk. Eat butter, bread (slowly baked, thoroughly done, eat fruits, good vegetables. And, stay away from lots of sweets, because sweets are dangerous. America has the record of eating more sweets than any other people.

Do not take chances, **period,** on your stomach. When it wears out, you are gone. You cannot replace stomachs.

The people suffer with so many sicknesses and diseases, due to the lack of care of what they put in their stomachs. There are many other things—the drink is included. Stay away from drinking that which you know is not good for you to drink.

Stay off of smoking tobacco in any form, or using it in any form. This shortens your life real fast, as God Taught me that it is like one in the back of the other one shooting him with a "45." If you notice, since nearly 40 years ago that I have been teaching you against smoking tobacco, the government almost hourly, everyday, is warning you against smoking. This is very good that they accept Divine Protection against the destruction of the human body.

LET US EAT TO LIVE AND NOT TO DIE.

CHAPTER FORTY FIVE

PROLONG YOUR LIFE

EAT one meal every twenty-four (24) hours, if you are not sick. Sometimes, when people are ill, in order to keep up their strength, they must eat.

THE HOLY QURAN, in teaching us to fast, says there is no particular regulation set upon those who are ill. The sick are not required to take a fast and this makes sense.

BUT, those of you who are well and able to withstand hunger; you will prolong your life by eating once a day, because it soon becomes a custom of ours, when we start eating, once a day. You do not hunger until that same time the next day.

We are the God of ourselves and we can make a habit of eating once every seven (7) days. We can train our bodies not to desire to take food, until the end of the seven (7) day period. We are just what we make of ourselves.

But you must remember, that food keeps us here and food takes us away. The longer we keep away from digging our graves with our teeth (as the old saying goes)...the longer we will live.

CHAPTER FORTY SIX

DO NOT NEED DRUGS IF WE LIVE RIGHT

This is one of the most important objects of our lives. How to eat to live, for Almighty God, Allah, in the Person of Master Fard Muhammad, to Whom praises are due forever, taught me that food keeps us here and food takes us away. So to regulate the food and drink is one of the important things of life.

TO EAT ONE meal a day and nothing between meals is driving away a lot of the 'cure all' drugs. We do not need drugs if we live right. In the next life, or under the rule of God, there will be no such thing as drugs to keep and maintain life.

Our enemies have resorted to drugs to prolong life, due to the fact that they do not want to accept the right way of God to prolong life over their commercial desire. Do you think doctors and drug scientists, who go out and look up chemicals for drugs to sell to you, want you to live without their profession by which they are making their living? I should say not.

To live without sickness is a very simple thing to do. Stop using the thing that makes us sick. We have been made so greedy it seems almost impossible for us to eat right and live a long life. But, it is easy when you begin it.

TO EAT TO LIVE does not mean that you will have a menu of various foods as long as your arm, from which to choose. You can eat one or two foods if you are not able to buy a lot of different foods, which will not destroy your life, such as good bread and pure milk and dried beans. This is sufficient to keep you living a thousand years.

Of course, a balanced diet is fine. In it you have plenty of garden vegetables with which you can change your diet, with or without eating that particular vegetable that will make you sick. But, one of the main things to prolong your life is to not eat too frequently.

Eat one meal a day. When you get used to eating one meal a day and you feel that you can eat one meal every two days without too many hunger pangs, then do so. Eat the food that I have been warning you to eat in this article for a long time.

Stay off hog flesh and essence. Do not say to me, "The white folks eat it and I don't see them dying so fast." Remember all that God says "Thou shall not do," the white man says "Thou shall do." He is a breaker of Divine law by nature and the greatest adversary of the Divine Supreme Being (made by nature to be so).

Eat to live and not to die, for food keeps you here and food takes you away. Eat one meal a day.

CHAPTER FORTY SEVEN

DOCTOR FALLS VICTIM
OF SAME SICKNESS

EAT ONE meal a day. Eat one meal every two days. Eat one meal every three days. Of whatever choice you take, it is going to help you, if you eat the right foods. This people (the white race) who have been our teacher in everything for 400 long years, did not teach us to eat right, because they were not eating right themselves. And, they, their children and their doctors all live about the same span of life. The span of life between the doctor and his patient is the same. Having a long life is the way we tell whether or not we are taught right in the way of prolonging our health.

LESSEN our sickness...the doctor falls victim of the same sickness and the same diseases as his patients and his span of life is the same as his patients. This professes beyond a shadow of a doubt that the doctor's teacher did not teach him right—how to live. You may like me to mention something? The white race did not try to persuade the doctor against alcoholic drinks and eating the pig and other stale meats of the land and the food of the sea. He teaches him to eat all the scavenger life of the sea that Muslims are turning down. And, the white man eats just the opposite of the way the righteous eat to keep the righteous from saying that he follows us. This is why the white man does not like us thinking against him and his own will. But, he must not do the same thing the righteous does, for the righteous will then tell him: "You were supposed to rule and teach the world that way, for our way will teach you of your ownself. Make a world of your own and do not follow ours to prove that you are good." And, this, he has done. Therefore, he went out eating all the filth and taught you to eat it. And, we who believed in his world and in his wisdom, fell for it. This is why all the judgment is here.

IF THE MEDICAL DOCTORS and the theologian teachers and scientists of   chemicals, are indulging and are not successful in expanding their own lives in what they are offering to us to eat and drink, then why should we follow their way of life? The chemical doctors go to the earth to get chemicals to heal them- selves and us..These chemicals soon will destroy both. And, their bodies were not made to be supported by chemicals for health and longevity. The fact is the body of man was not to be drugged. This white man brought all this "stuff" on us, because he was not going to be righteous, and he went to the earth to try to find a 'god' for his belly in drugs and chemicals. Now the 'thing' is catching up with him with what his own hands have produced. And they are willing to confess that these things are not good for us. They are turning down much of their medication, which is absolutely poison and detrimental to us. It is pro- phesied in the Holy Qur-an that when the God of Truth, Freedom, Justice, and Equality Comes, He Will Force this evil world to confess their evil. And, this, they are doing.

And, many of them are shocked over their own doings. And others are trying to teach you that their Brother is wrong.

I MET a priest a few years ago, and he told me out of his own mouth that he knew they have mistreated us and he hopes to do something about it. He looked very sick and very repentant. There are some white people who want to be good, but the essence that they are made of forces them to do otherwise. Therefore, the Bible warns us that a remnant of them will be saved.

WHAT WE EAT, AS GOD Taught me, keeps us here; and what we eat, takes us away. So, figure on what you will send down your throat, whether it will be something to keep you here or something to take you away. Some people love a lot of sweet and starchy foods. We should eat a little of both, but never to indulge in too much of it, it will start sugar boiling in your blood. Sugar can be controlled. It is not such a disease that cannot be controlled by your appetite. Just do not indulge in too much sugar. Eat a little bit.

IF YOU ARE a sugar diabetic, stay from sugar; for sugar will make you diabetic and you will never know that you have it until you indulge in too much sugar and starchy foods. Eat more protein foods. And eat more fish or that which water produces of life other than scavengers of the water. We have scavengers out there in the water and we have them on the land. Stay away from that kind of animal or life that lives on nothing but filth itself. And, do not be a slave to your eating desires. Be the master of what you should eat and do not allow the desire or hunger to be the master.

DO YOU THINK the old patriots who lived 500, 600, 700, 800, 900 and nearly 1,000 years ate such filth?

What do you think they ate? They did not eat your pig. They did not gobble down all kinds of meats and other foods three times a day. Some of them did not eat but one or two times a whole week. How do you think the people on Mars lived? "I do not know," you will say. And, they lived twelve hundred of our earth years. The Bible teaches us, and it is supposed to be from Jesus, that when God Comes, He comes to bring you life and take away death and give you more of abundance, plenty. He cannot do it without regulating our eating habits. So, this is the way to live a long time.

CHAPTER FORTY EIGHT

BEST PREVENTATIVE AGAINST DEATH

IT IS possible for us to eat many things and we can keep existing for a while, but if we would like to live as long as we CAN live, we need the proper guidance in the way of teaching us the proper foods to eat to expand our life and keep it expanded.

AS YOU KNOW, as I have repeatedly written in this book, that Allah (God) Taught me one meal a day of the right food will allow us to live a great, long while, even to 140 years and more, if we eat it once every other day and every three days instead of one meal every day.

WE ALL ARE very hesitant in refraining from eating food for any length of time. Why? It is because we are born eating all the food that we can get in our stomachs within one day. There is no regularity in this way of eating. We eat whenever we see some food. We are like pigs. The pig eats all of the time, so long as he sees food. And, we are like chickens and other fowl and animals that eat all of the time. Eating like this keeps our stomach churning to try to digest the food that we put in it, and to pass the food through to our intestines. This will soon wear the digestive juices of our stomach out and we only live as long as the stomach is capable of digesting what we put in it.

WE SUFFER with all kinds of ailments of the body, due to our own ignorant way of eating. How many times have you heard people say, when offered food, "do not wait until you are hungry, eat before you get hungry?'' This is a dangerous thing to follow, eating before you get hungry. I have heard many people, and you heard them say that they are eating just because they have not eaten in such a length of time or, "I missed my breakfast," or "I missed my lunch." They are eating then not because they are hungry, but they are eating because of the time they had set for themselves to eat.

THREE MEALS A DAY, within the short space of eight or ten hours could kill you at a very early age. All foods have a certain percentage of poison in it and if allowed to be increased in a very short while, then that keeps the body housing and storing up poison that it does not need to be housing; because we are making an addition to that already poison that is there. It makes sense. Sometimes this extra, unwanted food by the body, causes pain here and there; and we say that it is something else that it is coming from. It is that big meal that you are eating two and three times within eight or ten hours, or within twelve hours at the longest. So, we kill ourselves, as Allah (God) tells me; that there is no set time that we should die like our old parents were taught that when the time comes for you to die you will die regardless. Allah (God) told me there is no set time for us to die. We kill ourselves and that has been proven true.

WHEN WE get a pain, we run to the doctor for some drugs to stop it, or anything to stop the pain. If we had not found something to stop the pain, then maybe death would have come to us. But, seeing and knowing that death comes in the absence of a preventative against death, we should try and use the best preventative and that is to keep poison out of our bodies by abstaining from keeping our bodies stored with a lot of fresh food for it to digest.

CHAPTER FORTY NINE

SOME DOCTORS KNOW

Eat one meal a day or one meal every other day. You say: "Oh, I will starve if I eat like that; I have got to have my three meals.

THERE ARE even some professional people of ours such as doctors who know that this will prolong your life and theirs too, but they are like us, they were reared under the same teaching and therefore they cannot teach you what Allah Teaches us.

HOW TO EAT TO LIVE. It makes sense to wait such a length of time for our food to digest; it is good for us.

Do not be foolish to use such words as: "I cannot do that"..We can do many things. There are people known to go without food for forty days and nights. But, we have learned to be ever so eager to spend our language and time in foolishness.

We will feel better and we will keep the doctor away—not by an apple (smile), but by prolonging the time between each meal. I keep repeating to you, as others prophesied, that God Will Come to Give you life and more life, abundantly.

HE CANNOT give us more life if we hold on to death (eating without any regularity).

As the Holy Qur-an Teaches us, the devil eats as the beasts eat. There is no set time for the beast to eat. He eats whenever he sees his food present. This is the way many people are. They eat the food and will tell you, indirectly, "I said, I was not hungry." This is really ignorance. I said indirectly, but they tell you these things DIRECTLY.

There is hardly a one of you who does not wish to live a thousand years and who can hardly live a thousand days, the way you eat. You may say, "Well, how about you?" I am a man, according to the Bible, that is afflicted with everything that you are afflicted with. If I was not bearing the same affliction that you are afflicted with, maybe I would be better. But this affliction must come to me to prove that God and myself love you (that I am willing to go through with that which you are afflicted with, to bring you to a better way of life).

THE VERY EATING of one meal a day or one meal every other day makes your beauty appearance to shine more. You are the only people who do not need make up. You are already beautiful, by nature.

Stay away from all of his various kinds of foods and eat the common food. Do not try to eat all of that fancy food that he has your eyes attracted by and your appetite tempted by. This is not the kind of food that will make you live longer. But it is hard to get people like you away from that which is wrong and bad for your life.

The common food (just milk and bread or just bean soup and bread) is better than all the fancy food that you may try to eat. Eating good, common food will make you live a long time. This civilization intends to get us death and not long life. So, eat to live and not to die!

CHAPTER FIFTY
MEDICAL TEACHING BASED ON THREE MEALS A DAY

THIS world of the white race has hundreds and thousands of ways to tell you and to teach you how to eat. Please do not take up their many ways of HOW TO EAT—lest you do not have but one way to soon perish.

I GIVE you what I have received from Allah (God) Who Came in the Person of Master Fard Muhammad, to Whom Praises are due forever. He taught me that we eat one meal once every twenty-four (24) hours, a day—and nothing in between meals.

I HAVE tried this. I am one who has self-experience in this teaching and I have tried this world's way of eating, also.

EAT ONE MEAL PER DAY AND NOTHING BETWEEN MEALS, not even the drinking of milk, pops or juices. You must not eat or drink anything between meals. You must keep your stomach regulated to that one meal and when you drink enough water to digest that one meal, then do not drink any more water between meals.

PAY NO ATTENTION to your doctor saying that you need six (6) to eight (8) glasses of water with one meal per day. What he is telling you goes for three (3) meals per day. All of their medical teachings and administering is based upon a patient who eats three meals (3) per day.

AND we know what kind of health and sickness we had under such way of eating. This world offers you a thousand and one different kinds of food to eat. Do not let your eyes destroy your stomach. Eat that which is good and leave alone that which is not good for you. If you try to eat everything that probably is good for your stomach, you will soon have no stomach.

THE SIMPLE food is the food that will give us health; and not that food that we spice up with various kinds of spices. Neither is all that dainty meats, cakes and pies, good for you.

THE BIBLE warns us to be careful of the world's 'dainty meats' for the world worships the poison, filthy hog as their choice piece of meat. What Allah (God) Has Commanded, "Thou shalt not eat"; the wicked world says, "thou shalt eat."

FOR INSTANCE, most of the Muslims eat lamb (sheep). This world of the white race, found us on a diet of lamb, and they went for the cow, (beef) which is harder to digest than lamb flesh. Beef is coarser meat than lamb. Being coarser, it takes more of our stomach's digestive juices to digest it. And the cow is easily diseased.

SO they just eat the opposite of what Allah (God) gave us to eat and what they saw us eat. They adver- tise just the opposite food, which is against us.

EVEN TO the bread—they change it and they teach us that corn bread is good for us to eat. We can eat it if we have no other bread, but it is not good for us. If you eat corn bread you will wear your stomach out. It is too coarse for the stomach. They take the wheat flour and they ruin it by adding to it that which is not wheat. So do not look forward to their table for health-food, they do not have it.

LOOK at their advertisement of 'hot dogs'. For a man to hear that some food is named hot dogs, he would not want to eat it. The dog is a very filthy animal for one to name a food after. I do not see how in the world the public gets the idea to buy a food that goes under such a name as the filthy dog.

HOT DOGS—it is a very cheap food. It is made mostly of scrap beef—something that would not sell if the buyer or the consumer saw it before he bought it made into that fashion. Dog food! Hot dog—just think they buy this all over the world under that name.

THE most intelligent and delicate eater would not even buy a food that had such a name as 'hot dog'. They have certainly made fools of us. If the food is not dog, then why name it a dog?

WHY could not this food be named something that has a better meaning than to give it the name of the filthy dog,—hot dog?

I have worked in packing houses years ago and I have seen how these things, the hot dog, was made. I do not eat hot dogs myself. But after it is spiced up to taste good—and it is a little tasty but that does not mean that it is some fine beef flesh. No, that is not choice beef that the hot dog is made of.

WE CANNOT live eating any such food as that which is thrown on the market by the Christian world. They advertise that which Allah (God) Has already

Cursed from the beginning and they make us to eat the curse of Allah (God).

HOW TO EAT TO LIVE. Eat that food that Allah (God) Has Prescribed for us. Even take little simple things such as beans. Allah (God) says that the little navy bean will make you live, just eat them. He Said to me that even milk and bread would make us live. Just eat bread and milk—it is the best food. He Said that a diet of navy beans would give us a life span of one hundred and forty (140) years. Yet we cannot live one-half (½) that length of time eating everything that the Christian table has set for us.

VERY few Christians, even doctors, live eighty to ninety (80-90) years — not to think of living over one hundred (100) years. And they think they have lived for a long time if they reach a life span of eighty or ninety years. He has not been here long enough to know what life is.

NOAH and Methuselah lived almost into a thousand years, but we cannot live one-tenth (1/10) that time (100 years), because we eat the wrong food.

THE nature of this world (white man) was not to give and prolong our life; it is their nature to shorten our life, and they have done a good job of it. To destroy life is their very nature.

HOW TO EAT TO LIVE—eat simple food. Do not be reaching for all different kinds of food for they were prepared by the man who wants to commercialize on what you eat. They are interested in commerce. They eat the scavengers of the sea and the scavengers of the earth—reptiles and what not. They have no sense of choice—they will eat anything.

TRY and resort to what you find in this book and EAT TO LIVE.

CHAPTER FIFTY ONE

MANY AILMENTS CAN BE CURED

EAT one (1) meal per day and do not eat the food that you know is against you. If you do not know what foods are against you, please write to me and tell me what you are eating.

SUGAR—you eat too much sugar that is why we are troubled with diabetes. We eat too much starchy foods. Lay off of all those sugar and starchy foods and just eat common food.

EAT one (1) meal every twenty-four hours and if you do, you will write to me and tell me that you have been relieved of many of the ailments that you suffered with, while you were eating three (3) meals a day.

Lay off of drugs that are supposed to stimulate your appetite, and which cause you to over-eat.

IT IS unnecessary for you to try to eat, or even to taste all kinds of food. Eat the food that is good for you, then you will feel well, as a person should. Many of our ailments can be cured if we eat right. Stay away from drugs because the drugs themselves can kill you.

USE NO DRUGS to keep blood-sugar down. Just eat right. Stop eating sugar and starches and the sugar in your blood will clear up. I know because I have self-experience.

LAY off of starchy food and eat foods that contain protein.

DO NOT LET ANYONE TELL YOU THAT YOU CAN ENJOY GOOD HEALTH WHILE EATING THREE (3) MEALS PER DAY.

CHAPTER FIFTY TWO
NOT ALWAYS DOCTOR AND DRUG STORE BILLS

EAT JUST one (1) meal every twenty-four hours and do not go back with little snacks between meals. To do so is not eating one (1) meal a day.

BUT, if you are sick you are not required to follow the course of one (1) meal a day. But, if you are only sick with a greedy appetite, eat one (1) meal a day and you can control your sugar diabetes. You can also control little minor ailments such as all kinds of local fevers and diseases. By eating one (1) meal a day you will not attract minor ailments.

YOU will not have high fevers if you eat right and if you think right (a right heart). You CANNOT get good results from Allah's (God's) Law except that you think right. Your heart has to be in accord with what you say.

By eating one (1) meal a day, you will not be always paying doctor bills and drugstore bills for prescriptions. Eat one (1) meal a day and eat the proper food. Do not try to eat everything that is edible.

Just get yourself some common food. Number one, a bag of navy beans. Cook them well-done so that you will not get the colic from eating half-done beans. Put a little seasoning in the beans, if you want to. If you want meat in them, do not put pig in them. Use beef lamb or chicken in the pot of beans. Do not use fish to season the pot of beans.

EAT the beans and if you want something else,

like vegetables, eat the best of the vegetables that Allah (God) Has Caused to Grow out of the earth, for us.

BUT, do not eat leaf vegetable, such as collard greens, with some of us had taken for our diet. Do not eat a lot of green vegetables, anyway. Eat the white heads of vegetables, such as cauliflower and white heads of cabbage. Eat that type of food. You can eat the roots of turnips but do not eat the salad (leaves).

Eat rice, but do not eat the rice without washing it thoroughly until the water becomes clear as you pour it off the washed rice. And take the rice and parch it in a pan that has a little butter, vegetable oil or corn oil or olive in it. Keep turning the rice over in the pan and do not let it burn. Then put it into your boiler with water in it and let it boil slowly. Keep the fire low enough so that the water just pips. It does not take a lot of rapidly boiling water to cook rice. Just let it simmer on the stove until the grain of rice swells to two or three times its natural size.

THE LESS you eat the longer you live. You can eat once every two days. You will live that much longer. If you eat one meal a day from the cradle you should live three hundred (300) years or more, for you will not be sick, Allah (God) Who Came in the Person of Master Fard Muhammad, to Whom Praises are due forever Assured me of this.

YOU will not be sick often if you eat one (1) meal a day. And if you eat once every two (2) days you will not know what sickness feels like. That is if you eat the right food and the right food for thought thinking.

EAT right and abstain from eating when you are not hungry, and you will be able to do much in this world's life. I have tried all of these things so that I can know the results before I teach you to do for yourself and you may be happy.

STOP eating that three meals a day and eat one meal a day instead. Try out what Elijah teaches you for one week. See if you do not tell me that you are feeling better.

NEVER think to go near the hog and do not help prepare the hog for anyone else to eat. Do not even touch the hog. The hog is a very foul animal. Its name in Arabic is khanzier. The word khan-zier means, "I see foul and very foul."

THE HOG was made out of the cat, rat and dog, so Allah (God) Taught me. The hog has not always been on our planet earth. The hog was made for medical purposes, a few years after the making of the white race. He was made to cure the diseases that the white race attracts since they are physically weak, so Allah (God) Who Came in the Person of Master Fard Muhammad, to Whom Praises are due forever, Taught me, HOW TO EAT TO LIVE.

CHAPTER FIFTY THREE
DOCTORS LIVE SAME YEARS AS PATIENTS

HOW TO EAT TO LIVE is one of the number two Blessings that Allah (God) Who Came in the Person of Master Fard Muhammad To Whom Praises are due forever Has Brought to us. HOW TO EAT TO LIVE is the thing that everyone wants to know. Doctors who even study in order to learn what to teach their patients on how to live, they wind up living about the same number of years that their patients live. This goes to show that there is something wrong somewhere.

ALMIGHTY God, the Best Knower and the Wisest of Them all, did not teach me to eat a great variety of foods. Just common simple foods is what He dwelt upon, and finally He Said to me that bread and milk was enough and that it was the best of foods.

THE fact about it, milk is our first food—milk from our mother's breast. It used to be, but pride has taken away from the baby the milk that belonged to him—the milk from his mother's milk is better than the milk of a beast or cows' milk, for feeding the baby.

I lost a little nephew once, after my sister died, my mother tried to rear the baby on canned milk. We had no cow. That canned sweet milk constipated and killed that baby. So, when I married, I told my wife that I did not want her to try to rear her children on canned milk, and she agreed with me. She nursed her babies from her breast.

A baby nursed from its mother's breast will love its mother more than the baby fed from the bottle. He loves the bottle. When you feed the baby cow and other milk when it is in its infancy like that, the baby will be easy to be led by the animal. And if he knew that it was the animal or cattle's milk that is being fed to him, he will love that cattle instead of its mother, because any young will follow after that which feeds him. This is why the baby sometimes loves its nurse more than it loves its mother. It is because the baby's nurse feeds and cares for it.

IN this evil world, which is guilty of practicing every known evil, it does not teach you to practice to eat the right foods. Notice, the white race has all kinds of varities of foods to eat. It would kill dogs if you changed his diet to that which the white race eats. Soon you would have a dead dog.

JUST try giving the dog a lot of cakes and pies. Try and feed him walnuts, peanuts and all kinds of nuts. You will soon have no dog... You may say, "My dog eats peanut butter." No dog likes to eat a food that he cannot clean out of his mouth and into his stomach, quickly. Peanut butter is almost like glue. The dog has too hard a time getting the peanut butter out of its teeth.

AS I have said to you heretofore, that the reason the white race eats nuts it is due to them practicing eating this type of food four-thousand (4,000) years ago, when they were in the cave, before Moses brought them out of the cave.

CORN BREAD, Allah Taught me, should be cook-ed three or four times before we eat it. He Said to me, that it is best not to eat it at all. Never eat fresh bread, Brother. Bread just out of the oven is not good for you and me to eat. Let it stay over a day, at least and let it dry out. You should toast bread and almost burn it through. Regardless to what you do in the way of browning it, it will swell up in your stomach.

FISH is a better food, if you eat the better fish. The flesh of the fish comes out of another world. This makes it better for us in this world. Any animal or beast that is out here eating the same food that we eat, we should not eat him, because his flesh is too hard for our flesh to digest. All of our food in the way of meat should come from the sea, ocean, river or lakes, and not from four-footed animals that are walking around here and eating almost the same things that we are eating.

STAY well, eat simple foods and live a long time. In order to live a long time, eat simple foods and do not eat but one meal a day. Allah (God) Taught me, that in that way you will reach the age of 140 years. If you eat once every two (2) or three (3) days you could probably live like the old patriarchs, for nearly one-thousand (1,000) years.

I do not do all of these things (being restrictive about eating.) I act the fool sometimes. When I act the fool, I am learning more about you who are acting the fool and would think that you are pretty smart while it is death to you.

I did not say that it was really wrong for you to use alcohol. But it is wrong for you to use it in the way that you use it— getting drunk from alcohol. If we only know how to use anything with moderation, we would be a long time hurting ourselves.

TRY to eat all of your foods, fresh from the source from which it springs. In the frigid zone of the north, we have to can our food. But, if we can eliminate the canning idea and get our food fresh everyday, I say get your food everyday and eat it and what is left over, feed it to something else out here in the world and do not eat it tomorrow.

WE have a lot to talk about on the subject of HOW TO EAT TO LIVE. I have hardly scratched the surface.

Only eat one (1) meal a day and you will surely live long. Eat the proper food if you eat once, twice or three times a week. Do not say that you cannot eat once a week. It is the way that you train your stomach. You can make a habit of eating once every week and you will survive happily. So, EAT TO LIVE and not to die.

CHAPTER FIFTY FOUR
DESTROY SICKNESS AND DISEASE

PLEASE do not be mistaken about this teaching of HOW TO EAT TO LIVE, in a world in which you can get everything to eat, from the low and most unwanted creature of the earth, all the way back to human beings themselves. This world eats anything and everything. They eat both good foods and bad foods and they always try to establish some new food or new style of preparing new foods. Do not try to keep up with them in their way of teaching, lest you find yourself keeping up with them to the graveyard. You do not have to take anything that the white race says for truth. The answer can be found in our own lives— doctor and patient lived about an equal length of time. This shows that their way of teaching you and me, is that of "hill of mountain." You will not live as long as a hill or mountain. Your life is short and you follow their way. 75, 80, and 90 years is nothing to what you should be living, if you only knew the right kind of food that you should eat and abide by the rules and teachings of that type of food. We suffer with many ailments due to the improper foods and the improper time to eat. You have no regularity about when you are going to eat. Then your sickness — the consequences of an ignorant way of eating — will also have no regularity about it. The patient can be made to enjoy better health while having sickness and disease, if he eats at the proper time and eats the proper foods. Follow the right way of HOW TO EAT TO LIVE.

A HIGH percentage of blood sugar is a very dominate thing among the people but that blood sugar can be controlled, if you eat right. You will not even know that you had it, or that it is in you. We must eat the foods that will destroy sickness and disease.

CHAPTER FIFTY FIVE
DIGEST PROPERLY

If we expect to live from what we eat, we must be sure that what we eat is masticated so perfectly well, until the stomach juices (which have no teeth), with its hot acid can digest the food without too much work.

THE AMERICAN EATERS, I believe, when it comes to a human being, are the fastest of all on the earth in eating their food.

On many work jobs, they are only allowed 15, 20, and 30 minutes to eat their food. Here goes food down the throat in wads that have never been chewed as it should; not allowing it any time to take on the nature (saliva) which attacks our food at entering of the mouth, to try to help it to go down to the stomach.

All through our food's travel down the throat, it is being sprayed with this saliva. And, down in the organ of our stomach (which scientists say holds about a pint and a half of fluids), it is processed again with the same digestive juices which are a little stronger than that they get, coming into this organ. Then, it takes on a dash of gall, and is distributed throughout our small intestinal area to the big colon that looks like a frame running down from the right to the left.

TO HASTEN OUR MEALS down in these areas, that were mentioned, that make up the machination of our digestive system, half masticated, puts too much labor on this machination of our bodies and causes sores in the stomach and in the intestinal tract, that we refer to as ulcers and from ulcers to cancers. (I want you to see how we destroy our own body).

185

A man should chew his food (as many doctors teach us and agree with what is said here), until it slips away into the throat, before swallowing.

This is America's number one cause of her many ailments coming to her (fast eating; half chewing her food) and eating half done foods such as half done peas and half done lima beans and all kinds of beans and half done meats and bread. Take bread, for an instance, when it is not baked thoroughly done and has not been given time to dry out for a day or two (of which the foolish call it stale bread, after it leaves the oven if it stays there a day or two). The scientists have proven there is no such thing as stale bread. When the bread is old and creating what they call mold; that is your best bread.

All of your trouble; hospitalization; and bad stomachs—caused from fast eating and bad food.

YOU MUST REMEMBER when you are eating bread, when it gets into your stomach it rises again, and, if it is not prepared right and baked right outside, before entering our stomach, it has the tendancy to buckle in the stomach and intestines. But, when it is baked thoroughly done, it does not do a lot of rising after it gets into our stomach.

Bake your bread thoroughly done!! I would to my Allah, we could eat bread that has been baked two or three times.

Chew all of your food slowly and eat only one meal per day, if you are well. If you are sick, that is different. You will find yourself not having doctors to roll you into hospitals to cut away your stomach of ulcers and cancers and your years will be longer.

Oh! you "sweet tooths;" stay off of that sugar and those sweets (bread, cakes, icings and what not)... You are only killing yourself and happy to do so, because of the taste of sugar. Please remember this, eat to live, not to die.

HOW TO EAT TO LIVE.

CHAPTER FIFTY SIX

LONG INTERVALS BETWEEN EATING IS BETTER

The great trouble the people have trying to keep in good health is the enemy who is poisoning food and drinks.

HOW CAN people enjoy good health while eating poison deliberately prepared and put into their food and drinks to shorten their lives?

It is very hard to find anything like pure food and drinks which you can eat and drink without feeling that they are going to make you sick or kill you.

TAKING long intervals between eating meals makes it better for you, because long intervals between meals and drinks give the poison in the body time to weaken before a new addition of poisonous food and drinks.

They do not mind hiding their intention to use poison, for they know that it will have an effect upon your body and your enjoyment of good health.

YOU could not imagine a more wicked thing to do than for someone to take a good food for innocent people—from the cradle to old age—and poison it so that the eater and the drinker cannot enjoy good health and will be at the hospital doorstep where they will be denied immediate service (especially so-called Negroes).

I have, for years, advised you on the South Side here in Chicago to let us unite and build a hospital large enough to take care of our sick, because they surely will be sick, as long as they live in a world that specializes on how to make one sick (sometimes just for commercial purposes, so doctors can make more money and so undertakers can make more money).

MORE white and Black scientists agree that America is a very poisonous place to live today. The poisoning of food and drinks is done deliberately and there is no help coming from the government to stop such demoniac, evil freedom to maim and destroy life.

Our only hope for survival is in Allah, Who has power over the evil plans of the devil.

CHAPTER FIFTY SEVEN
AN ECONOMIC PLAN FOR ALL

Let it be known that the "Three-Year Economic Plan" is for ALL 22 MILLION OF THE SO-CALLED AMERICAN NEGROES for the purpose of helping self against poverty and want and to curtail our wild and wasteful spending.

If all of the money spent in a year by our people for beer, soda water, wine and whiskey were put together, your eyes would bulge to see the amount wasted. Let us add cigarettes and tobacco to the list of wasteful spending, taking more wealth from an already poor and impoverished people. Then, let us include the poison hog meat to the list —which we can definitely do without—because, along with tobacco, it destroys our good health.

If you stopped eating the poison hog, the devils probably would give it to you, because they want you to have that which is detrimental to your good health. There is plenty of beef, fish and chicken for you to eat. So, why fill your bodies with poisonous foods, which produces complaints throughout your life—and shortens it as well? Ask the medical scientists if you do not believe men.

Why not send all of that money to me, so I can build a bank full of millions of dollars to keep you from begging for a house in which to live, and food and clothing for yourself and family? Learn to save and to do for self, instead of learning to be a slave for others and doing for them.

If you are just able to give a nickel, let us put it up for you in savings, to help buy our food, clothing and shelter; to start farming and building factories and plants like those possessed by other nations. We are wasting our time and education, and even unity, because we want to do everything for others but nothing for self, while hoping someone else will help us.

If you will send your money to OUR (yours and mine) "Three-Year Savings Plan," we can build a future for ourselves. We must have land of our own.

I EXPECT YOUR CONTRIBUTIONS IN THE NEXT MAIL.

INDEX

INDEX

194

INDEX

INDEX

INDEX

INDEX

INDEX

INTRODUCING...

THE THREE YEAR ECONOMIC PROGRAM

The **THREE YEAR ECONOMIC PROGRAM** launched by the **Honorable Louis Farrakhan** on October 7, 1991 is designed to address the critical needs of the Black community in the upcoming years.

Your monthly contribution will help to establish farms and businesses that will meet the necessities of life and lay the foundation for our economic survival.

Send your $10 monthly donation to:

THE THREE YEAR ECONOMIC PROGRAM

4855 South Woodlawn Avenue Chicago, Illinois 60615

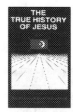

Muhammad University *of* Islam

7351 South Stony Island Avenue
Chicago, Illinois 60649

SUPPORT
YOUR OWN INDEPENDENT EDUCATIONAL INSTITUTION!

Under the leadership of The Honorable Louis Farrakhan, the Muhammad University of Islam opened to the public on September 6, 1989, including a licensed Early Childhood Learning Center for children ages 2 to 4 years old, and kindergarten to 12th grades. Founded by the Honorable Elijah Muhammad to re-educate our nation into the rich knowledge of self.

We need your financial support to purchase school buses and equipment, and to complete our library and science lab. We acknowledge with deepest gratitude all contributions previously made.

All donations may be mailed to:
**THE HONORABLE ELIJAH MUHAMMAD
EDUCATIONAL FOUNDATION**
c/o Sister Tynetta Muhammad (President)
4855 South Woodlawn Avenue
Chicago, Illinois 60615
MAY ALLAH RICHLY REWARD YOUR EFFORTS

Personally-autographed poster of
Minister Louis Farrakhan

11^{50}

18" X 24"
glossy color

Your contribution helps to further the progress of Minister Farrakhan in continuing the work of The Honorable Elijah Muhammad

Name: ....

Address: ....

City/State/Zip: ....

Make your check or money order payable to:
No. 2 Poor Treasury.
Mail to:
Minister Louis Farrakhan,
c/o 4855 South Woodlawn Avenue
Chicago, Illinois 60615

FINAL CALL INC. BOOKS AND TAPES

 ORDER FORM

Qty	Audio	Video	Book	Title	Unit Price	Total Price
	Check One			**Please Print**		

Name_____

Address _____

City/State/Zip _____

Phone _____

SUBTOTAL	
SHIPPING	
TOTAL	

Check one: VISA ☐   MASTERCARD ☐   Exp. Date: _____

Please make check or money order payable to : **FINAL CALL** and mail to **FINAL CALL INC.**, 734 W. 79th Street, Chicago Il.,60620. Incude $3.00 for shipping and handling and .50 cents for each additional item. Please allow four weeks for delivery. Wholesale orders are accepted. *Check orders take 14 days before processing; money orders are recommended.*

THE
MUSLIM PROGRAM

What The Muslims Want

This is the question asked most frequently by both the whites and the blacks. The answer to this question I shall state as simply as possible.

1. We want freedom. We want a full and complete freedom.

2. We want justice, Equal justice under the law. We want justice applied equally to all, regardless of creed class or color.

3. We want equality of opportunity. We want equal membership in society with the best in civilized society.

4. We want our people in America whose parents or grandparents were descendants from slaves, to be allowed to establish a separate state or territory of their own-either on this continent or elsewhere. We believe that our former slave masters are obligated to provide such land and that the area must be fertile and minerally rich. We believe that our former slave masters are obligated to maintain and supply our needs in this separate territory for the next 20 to 25 years until we are able to produce and supply our own needs.

Since we cannot get along with them in peace and equality, after giving them 400 years of our sweat and blood receiving in return some of the worst treatment human beings have ever experienced, we believe our contributions to this land and the suffering forced upon us by white America, justifies our demand for complete separation in a state or territory of our own.

5. We want freedom for all Believers of Islam now held in federal prisons. We want freedom for all black men and women now under death sentence in innumerable prisons in the north as well as in the south.

We want every black man and woman to have the freedom to accept or reject being separated from the slave masters children and establish a land of their own.

We know that the above plan for the solution of the black and white conflict is the best and only answer to the problem between two people.

6. We want an immediate end to the police brutality and mob attacks against the so-called Negro throughout the United States.

We believe that the federal government should intercede to see that black men and women tried in white courts receive justice in accordance with the laws of the land-or allow us to build a new nation for ourselves, dedicated to justice freedom and liberty.

7. As long as we are not allowed to establish a state or territory of our own, we demand not only equal justice under the laws of the United States, but equal employment opportunities-NOW!

We do not believe that after 400 years free or nearly free labor, sweat and blood, which has helped America become rich and powerful, that so many thousands of black people should have to subsist on relief, charity or live in poor houses.

8. We want the government of the United States to exempt our people from ALL taxation as long as we are deprived of equal justice under the laws of the land.

9. We want equal education-but separate schools up to 16 for boys and 18 for girls on the condition the girls be sent to women's colleges and universities. We want all black children educated, taught and trained by their own teachers.

Under such schooling system we believe we will make a better nation of people. The United States government should provide, free, all necessary text books and equipment, schools and college buildings, The Muslim teachers shall be left free to teach and train their people in the way of righteousness, decency and respect.

10. We believe that intermarraige of race mixing should be prohibited. We want the religion of Islam taught without hinderance or supression.

These are some of the things that we, the Muslims, want for our people in North America.

What The Muslims Believe

1. WE BELIEVE in One God whose proper name is Allah.

2. WE BELIEVE in the Holy Qur'an and in the scriptures of all the prophets of God.

3. WE BELIEVE in the truth of the bible, but we believe that it has been tampered with and must be reinterpreted so that mankind will not be snared by the falsehoods that have been added to it.

4. WE BELIEVE in Allah's prophets and the Scriptures they brought to the people.

5. WE BELIEVE in the ressurection of the dead-not in physical resurrection-but mental resurrection. We believe that the so-called Negroes are most in need of mental resurrection; therefore, they will be resurrected first.

Furthermore, we believe we are the people of God's choice, as it has been written, that God would choose the rejected and the despised. We can find no other persons fitting this description in these last days more than the so-called Negroes in America. We believe in the resurrection of the righteous.

6. WE BELIEVE in the judgement; we believe this first judgement will take place as God revealed, in America...

7. WE BELIEVE this is the time in history for the separation of the so-called Negroes and the so-called white Americans. We believe the black man should be freed in name as well as in fact. By this we meanthat he should be freed from the name imposed upon him by his former slave masters. Names which identified him as being the slave masters slave. We believe that if we are free indeed, we should go in our own people names the black people of the earth.

8. WE BELIEVE in justice for all, whether in God or not; we believe as others, that we are due equal justice as human beings.We believe in equality-as a nation-of equals.We do not believe that we are equal with our slave masters in the status of "freed slaves".

We recognize and respect American citizens as independent peoples and we respect their laws which govern this nation.

9. WE BELIEVE that the offer of intergration is hypocritcal and is made by those who are trying to deceive the Black peoples into believing that their 400 year-old openenemies of freedom, justice and equality are, all of a sudden, their "friends". Furthermore, we believe that such deception is intended to prevent Black people from realizing that the time in history has arrived for the separation from the whites of this nation.

If the white people are truthful about their professed freindship toward the so-called Negro, they can prove it by dividing up America with their slaves.

We do not believe that America will be able to furnish enough jobs for her own millions of unemployed, in addition to jobs for the 20,000,000 Black people as well.

10. WE BELIEVE that we who declare ourselves to be righteous Muslims, should not participate in wars which take the lives of humans. We do not believe this nation should force us to take part in such wars, for we have nothing to gain from it unless America agrees to give us the necessary territory wherein we may have something to fight for.

11. WE BELIEVE our women should be respected and protected as the women of other nationalities are respected and protected.

12. WE BELIEVE that Allah (God) appeared in the Person of Master W. Fard Muhammad, July, 1930; the long-awaited "Messiah" of the Christians and the "Mahdi" of the Muslims.

We believe further and lastly that Allah is God and besides HIM there is no God and He will bring about a universal government of peace wherein we all can live in peace together.